B122 An introduction to retail management and marketing

Book 3
Retail marketing

Prepared by Fiona Ellis-Chadwick

START 3

This publication forms part of the Open University module B122 *An Introduction to Retail Management and Marketing*. Details of this and other Open University modules can be obtained from the Student Registration and Enquiry Service, The Open University, PO Box 197, Milton Keynes MK7 6BJ, United Kingdom (tel. +44 (0)845 300 60 90; email general-enquiries@open.ac.uk).

Alternatively, you may visit the Open University website at www.open.ac.uk where you can learn more about the wide range of modules and packs offered at all levels by The Open University.

To purchase a selection of Open University module materials visit www.ouw.co.uk, or contact Open University Worldwide, Walton Hall, Milton Keynes MK7 6AA, United Kingdom for a brochure (tel. +44 (0)1908 858793; fax +44 (0)1908 858787; email ouw-customer-services@open.ac.uk).

The Open University Walton Hall, Milton Keynes MK7 6AA

First published 2011

Edited and designed and typeset by The Open University.

Printed in the United Kingdom by Cambrian Printers, Aberystwyth.

ISBN 978 1 7800 7312 5

2.1

Contents

Introduction to Book 3	5
Session 2 Retail marketing planning	7
2.1 What is retail marketing planning?	7
2.2 Business mission	12
2.3 Marketing audit	13
2.4 SWOT analysis	15
2.5 Marketing objectives	17
2.6 Core strategy	22
2.7 Competitive advantage	23
2.8 Marketing mix decisions	25
2.9 Evaluating the marketing strategy	28
2.10 Organisation, implementation and control	28
2.11 Conclusions	30
Session 3 Consumer behaviour	32
3.1 Who is important in the buying decision?	33
3.2 How do people buy and what choice criteria do they use?	35
3.3 Influences on consumers' purchasing	43
3.4 Conclusions	46
Session 4 Retail brands	47
4.1 What is a brand?	48
4.2 Growth of retailer own-label brands	50
4.3 Types of retail brands	58
4.4 Retail brands and own-label brands	60
4.5 Conclusions	80
Block 3 Conclusions	81
References	82
Ailawadi and Keller references	83
Acknowledgements	89
Module team	91

Introduction to Book 3

Welcome to Book 3, where we are continuing to explore retailing from a marketing perspective. Marketing is a highly dynamic and challenging part of retail activity and success in this arena can be affected by the ever-changing trading environment and the management expertise at store level. Nevertheless, retailers using marketing techniques have created some world-renowned brands and have often achieved such status through innovation and the adoption of creative marketing management techniques. This book builds on your work in the multimedia activities where you have studied the 'retail marketing mix' by focusing on marketing planning and the associated topics of consumer behaviour and branding.

There are three study sessions in this book:

Session 2 Retail marketing planning

Session 3 Customer behaviour

Session 4 Retail brands.

As with Blocks 1 and 2, we continue to provide theoretical insights and practical case illustrations but in this block we focus on the fundamental principles of retail marketing. You have already encountered various different examples of how retailers use the marketing communication mix in the online session in the VLE. Now you are going to explore how all of the elements of marketing are drawn together to create a coherent plan which can give a retailer strategic direction. By the end of the book you will also have discovered the importance of consumer behaviour and identified the key components of building a brand, which is an important part of retail success for every retailer from the independent to the multinational retailer.

Customers are individuals who shop at a particular store. Consumers are the wider pool from which customers might be drawn

These images show two very different retailers, Montague Jefferies an independent specialist menswear retailer and Clarks, a multinational specialist footwear retailer. Think for a moment what might be important to each of these retailers in terms of positioning their brand in the marketplace. Both retailers believe excellent customer service is a top priority and provide high quality goods for sale. Each retailer also has a story – their brand heritage – which gives consumers of each brand the confidence to become repeat customers. You will learn more about how retailers develop themselves as brands later in this book.

In addition to the printed and online module materials, there is a tutor group forum (TGF) activity at the end of this book. It is important to take part in this activity as it should help your understanding of retail marketing management issues and give you an opportunity to learn about the viewpoints of others. Perhaps most importantly it is an opportunity for you to secure easy marks towards your assessment for Block 3.

Learning outcomes

The aims of Book 3 are to provide you with a broad understanding of the marketing planning process and the importance of the consumer decision making process to retail marketing planning and to explain the core concepts of retail branding.

More specifically the learning outcomes for this block are to:

- investigate the process of consumer buying and develop an understanding of the importance of consumer behaviour to retail marketing managers
- learn about the basic principles of retail branding
- identify the stages in the marketing planning process
- consider each of the elements of the retail marketing mix
- explore elements of the communication process.

Session 2 Retail marketing planning

This session will look at the importance of marketing planning from the retailers' perspective. The aim is to describe the role of marketing planning within retailing and to discuss the planning process.

2.1 What is retail marketing planning?

Marketing is more than advertising, cut-price promotions and smart-talking sales people. Marketing is about understanding how to create customer value and then planning to achieve market-focused goals. Retailers need customers to return and make repeat purchases: 'the goal of marketing is long-term satisfaction not short-term deception' (Jobber, 2010, p. 3).

Therefore, for a retailer to successfully plan and adopt a marketing orientation they must understand that it is a guiding philosophy which influences every aspect of the organisation. This means that all operations are devised to support the creation of customer satisfaction; all staff throughout the company must recognise the importance of customer satisfaction and as a result accept responsibility for creating customer satisfaction; and finally there must be a belief throughout the company that the retailer's goals can be achieved through customer satisfaction. In other words, marketing includes the whole of the retail operation from the products for sale to dealing with complaints, the buying function, the logistics department and much more.

As you develop your marketing knowledge, it is important to be able to differentiate between companies and organisations which adopt a marketing orientation and those driven by different orientations, for example production orientation.

Marketing-orientated companies get close to their customers so that they understand their needs and problems and as a result the business is market driven. This type of organisation will focus its efforts on developing strategies which maximise the benefits to the customer, identifying potential market opportunities, and then developing products and services which meet these opportunities and in doing so satisfy customer needs.

Production-orientated companies focus on production methods before thinking about the customer. Managers of this type of company become cost focused, believing that the main management function is to attain economies of scale by producing a limited range of products in a form that minimises production costs. An aggressive sales effort is used to sell products regardless of the benefits to the buyer.

Activity 2.1 Adopting a market orientation

Spend about 10 minutes on this activity.

Purpose: to consider the difference between product and marketing orientations.

Task: Using your knowledge and experience, identify an example of a market-orientated retailer and give examples to support your choice. Then suggest indicators which help identify market-orientated retailers.

Feedback

My example is McDonald's, the world's most well-known fast-food operation, which primarily sells products high in calories and fat content, for example, hamburgers, French fries, sugary drinks and desserts. However, in recent years, the company has adapted its menus to include healthier alternatives such as salads and fresh fruit in response to consumer demand in countries in Europe and North America, where obesity is a problem.

Thinking of indicators of market-orientated retailers is not easy. It requires you to apply the knowledge you have acquired about how to develop customer-focused retail operations. You could have suggested any of the following indicators:

- gathering customer data in a variety of ways, for example, in store, online or by post
- face-to-face interactions with customers by retail staff, for example, at a customer service desk
- a customer complaint handling service and rectification of service failures
- trained staff who are able to answer customer enquiries and deal with customer complaints
- internal communications and training to inform staff of changing customer policies
- responsiveness to market trends, for example, adaptive pricing strategies in changing economic circumstances.

Retailers have not always adopted a market orientation and practised marketing management. Development of marketing as an important part of marketing has taken many decades.

The development of retail marketing

The marketing mix is considered to encompass four key business areas which influence marketing planning: product, price, place and promotion.

During the last few decades, significant changes in retailing have led to major retailers dominating marketing channels and accruing power over manufacturers and wholesalers. This has largely come about as retailers have progressively taken control of more and more elements of the marketing mix (McGoldrick, 2002, p. 2).

In the past, retailing was depicted as taking a largely passive role in the distribution process: goods passed from the manufacturer to the consumer through the retailer. The retailer then had to attempt to sell products made available by the manufacturer. However, according to (McGoldrick, 2002, p. 2) this manufacturer-centred view of distribution channels has seriously understated the power, scope and importance of retail marketing. Now it is realistic to talk of 'channels of supply' whereby the retailer is actively involved throughout the supply chain and adopts a market-centred view.

The shift in the balance of power from manufacturer to supplier and then retailer occurred from the early 1970s, when there was a major shift in channel power. Post-war shortages in the 1950s gave manufacturers the edge so this was an era when the 'manufacturer was king'. By the 1960s, consumer spending was on the increase, as was competition. There was a noticeable shift towards the consumer, so in this era the customer was king. However, by the 1970s trade became more concentrated and powerful retailer corporations increasingly took over the functions of marketing so in this era 'trade was king' (McGoldrick, 2002, p. 2).

However, there was more to the retailer's marketing success than just taking over control of the supply chain. Major multiple retailers, for example, Walmart, Carrefour, Tesco and Sainsbury's, constantly develop market share through better understanding of the customer and tailoring their business to satisfy customer needs.

Retailers also developed power in the supply chain through:

- the abolition of resale price maintenance (RPM) and the development of strong retailer brands
- the concentration of retail trading – in other words, market-leading brands dominating various sectors, e.g., Toys'R'us (toys category)
- terms of trade, for example, large retailers leveraging power by using their greater purchasing power over smaller retailers
- access to information brought about by retailers' widespread use of data capture technology.

The shift in the balance of power between retailers and manufacturers led to increasing dependence on the multiple retailers, which facilitated the growth of this type of retailer. This trend has continued to the present day and a small number of very large retailers dominate many retail sectors both nationally and globally. Examples include:

Retailer	Region	Sector
Walmart Stores, Inc.	USA	Discount store
Carrefour Group	France	Hypermarkets
The Home Depot	USA	Home improvement
Metro AG	Germany	Diversified
Tesco Plc	UK	Supermarkets

However, even though retailers gained power over the marketing mix many failed to apply marketing in a coordinated and comprehensive manner. Rather, they tended to use elements of the mix but lacked organisation and coordination.

Eventually, retailers began to realise the strategic importance of marketing and by the 1980s most major retailers had a marketing department (Piercy and Alexander, 1988). Since then retailers have developed sophisticated marketing solutions to deal with an increasingly complex and demanding marketing environment. Furthermore, the demand for an increasing range of managerial skills and competencies has created a new breed of retailing professionals, who are adept at market analysis, strategic thinking and planning (McGoldrick, 2002, p. 8–9).

Indeed, Jennison wrote:

> The retail sector has some of the most innovative and successful companies in the world, yet it is only recently that retailing has become recognised as a true profession.
>
> (Jennison, 1997)

In the twenty-first century, retailers have not only realised the importance of marketing principles to the success of their operations but have also developed skills and knowledge which enable them to lead the development of marketing in practice. This shift towards adoption of a marketing orientation means the role of customers is very important and their needs are placed at the heart of marketing planning.

The remainder of Session 2 explores the marketing planning process.

The retail marketing planning process

According to Jobber, there are six fundamental questions which form the starting point for the planning process. The questions are:

1. Where are we now?
2. How did we get here?
3. Where are we heading?
4. Where would we like to be?

5. How do we get there?
6. Are we on course?

(Jobber, 2010, pp. 38–9)

By answering each of these questions, a business can develop a marketing plan.

The stages in the marketing planning process are shown in Figure 2.1. This model is useful as it provides a clearly defined path from the vision of what a business might be to the actual implementation. However, you must be aware that in the real world of business, planning and implementation rarely follow such well-ordered stages. Often many stages of the plan are being worked on simultaneously and events occur which require immediate changes. Nevertheless, this structured approach to marketing planning is useful as it shows:

1 a systematic way of getting to know about each of the elements of the planning process
2 how individual elements of the planning process are integrated.

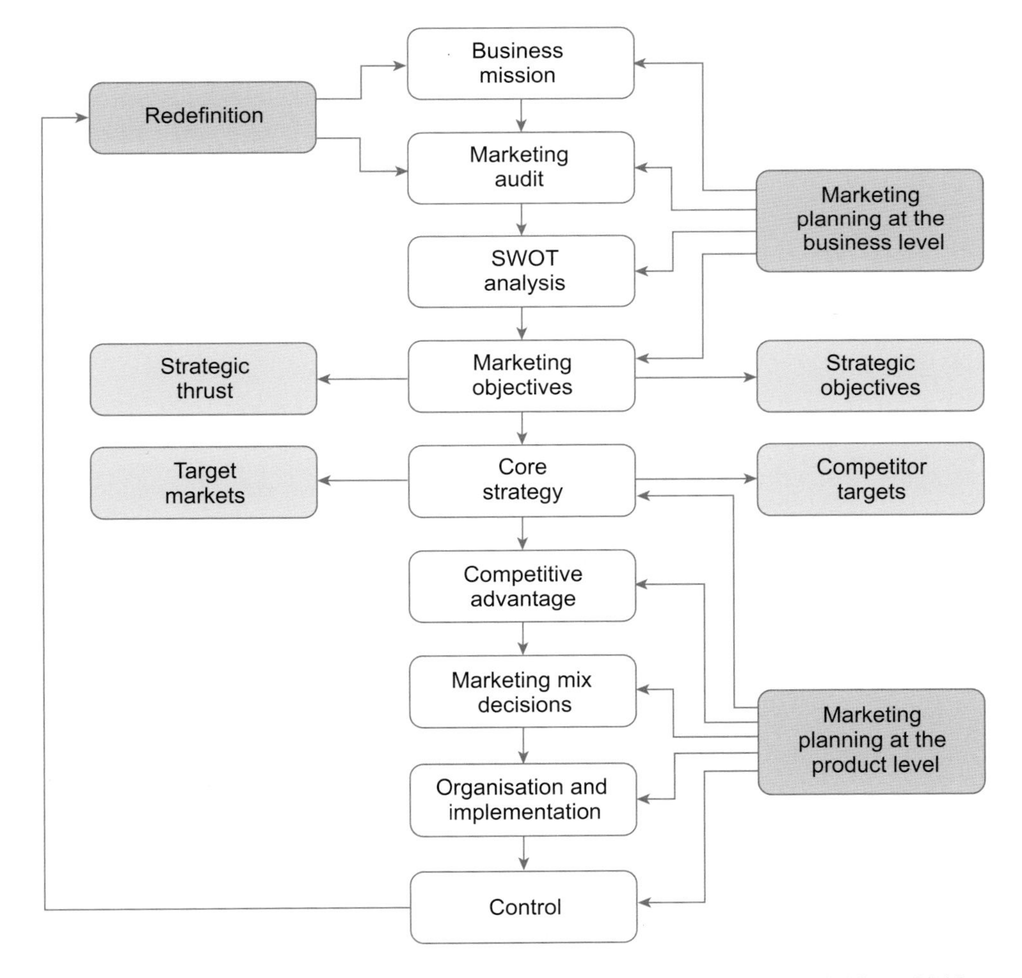

Figure 2.1 The stages in the marketing planning process (Source: Jobber, 2010, p. 40).

Activity 2.2 Stages in planning a journey

Spend about 10 minutes on this activity.

Purpose: to reflect on your personal approach towards planning.

Task: Imagine you need to make a journey and list the stages you might go through when planning the trip.

Feedback

An early stage in your planning is likely to be to establish the purpose of the trip – for example, business trip, pleasure outing with family, visit to a doctor, shopping excursion, holiday – as this will help to set many parameters for the journey such as timing, duration, cost, urgency.

If your journey is for pleasure you are likely to 'audit' your resources again to help you identify possible options. When planning a holiday, you may think about previous experiences, available finance, who else might take the trip.

Having gathered information you are likely to evaluate the alternatives and set some goals for the journey. For example, on a shopping excursion you may want to buy a specific item or you may intend to have a day out socialising with a friend in the city's retail district.

Our personal planning tends to be less structured, complex or controlled than a business's marketing plan but I hope you can appreciate that there are stages in the planning process which inform how decisions are made.

We will now consider each of the stages in Figure 2.1 and their implications for retailers in the marketing planning process.

2.2 Business mission

A business should have a mission statement which guides all its activities.

In 1976 Dame Anita Roddick opened her first shop, called The Body Shop, in Brighton selling cosmetics. The company grew rapidly and by 1985 it became a public company. In 2010, The Body Shop had over 2,400 stores and franchises in over 60 countries around the world. Roddick wanted to develop a business that was socially responsible and the mission statement, which continues to guide the company's development, is: 'to dedicate our business to the pursuit of environmental change' (Dennis et al., 1997 pp. 649–53).

This mission statement has proved to be enduring and has served to distinguish the business from its competitors. It is important to be aware these are the two essentials of a mission statement (Ackoff, 1987). In other words, it is important for retailers to develop a mission statement which sets out the business they are in and the reason for the existence of the business.

A business mission provides focus for developing other stages of the marketing planning process but it is important to understand that the guiding mission has to be operationalised in order to deliver business success and to achieve this the retailer should understand the trading environment. In Block 1 you explored the forces which shape the trading environment. In the marketing planning process, conducting a marketing audit enables you to capture how those forces are, or might be, affecting a retail business.

The Body Shop sources all of the cocoa needed in its cosmetics from Kuapa Kokoo under the Community Trade Initiative as this helps ensure company actions align with its business mission.

2.3 Marketing audit

The marketing audit provides a framework for a systematic examination of a business's marketing environment and sets out the basis for the development of the marketing plan. The audit helps to identify key problem areas and provides the means to answer the first three of our key planning questions: Where are we now? How did we get here? Where are we heading?

In order to answer these questions, we need to analyse the marketing environment, which you studied in Block 1.

Activity 2.3 The marketing environment

Spend about 10 minutes on this activity.

Purpose: to review your learning about the marketing environment.

Task:

(a) Name the five broad macro-environment forces that can affect a business.

(b) Name the five elements which make up the micro-environment.

(c) What is the main difference between the macro-environment and the micro-environment?

(d) What are demographics?

(e) When a company investigates the extent to which it can use recyclable and non-wasteful packaging, which environmental force is it responding to?

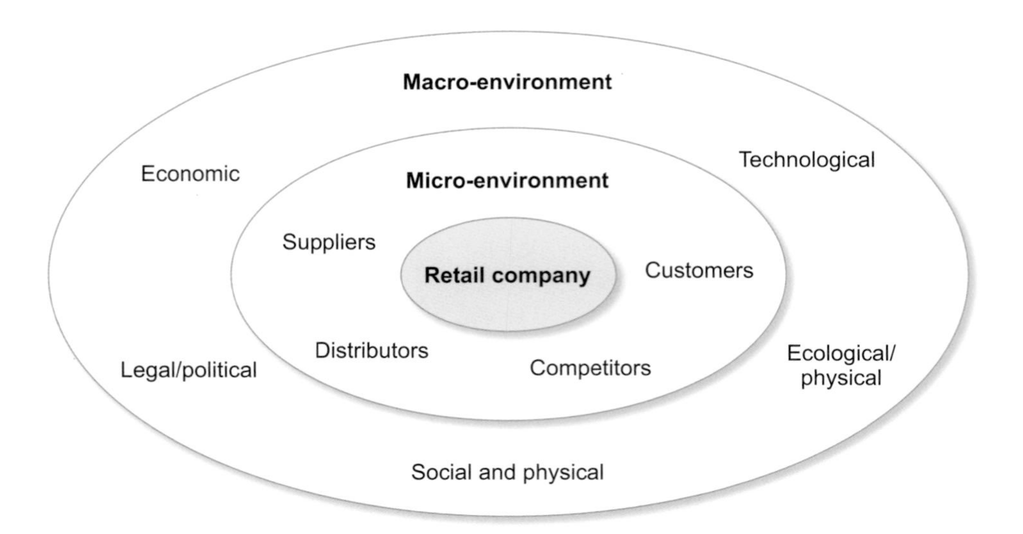

This diagram from Book 1 showing the retail environment is repeated as an *aide-memoire* to help you with this activity.

Feedback

(a) Political, economic, social, technological and ecological.

(b) Market, customers, competitors, distributors and suppliers.

(c) The macro-environment consists of forces which can affect business performance. The micro-environment consists of the actors in a business's immediate environment which affect its ability to operate effectively.

(d) Demographics/demography is the study of changes in world population, age distribution and household incomes. Marketers frequently use demographics to inform targeting and marketing planning decisions.

(e) Ecological.

Identifying the elements of the micro- and macro-environment (or the internal and external environment) helps to provide us with a checklist of the issues a retailer might consider when conducting a marketing audit. Remember how we explored the elements of the environment in Block 1, now you can see how this understanding helps with marketing planning.

The external audit focuses on reviewing the forces in the environment which can affect business performance, whilst the internal audit focuses on the business's activities.

> An internal marketing audit checklist means focusing on company performance in terms of: *operating results*, for example, sales, market share, profit margins and costs; *market mix effectiveness*; *strategic performance*, for example marketing objectives, target markets, competitive advantage; product portfolio; *marketing structures*, for example, organisation of marketing within the company; training; departmental communications; *marketing systems*, for example, information, planning and control.
>
> (Jobber, 2010, p. 44)

A marketing audit should be conducted in a timely manner not as a reaction to an event in the external or internal environment. Ideally, it is an ongoing activity, which is used to support business planning and decision making. The audit should enable a company to evaluate its current position. The next stage in the planning process is to consider where the company is heading and where it would like to be heading. This can be achieved by identifying the positives and negatives which are likely to affect future successes.

2.4 SWOT analysis

A marketing audit is a process of constant information gathering and analysis. But the information and intelligence created by the audit need to be summarised so they can be used to inform the development of a marketing plan. One way to achieve this is to conduct a SWOT analysis.

SWOT stands for Strengths, Weaknesses, Opportunities, and Threats and is a widely used structured approach to analysing the output of the marketing audit. The SWOT analysis provides a straightforward way of identifying key planks that can be used to form the basis of a marketing plan (see Figure 2.2).

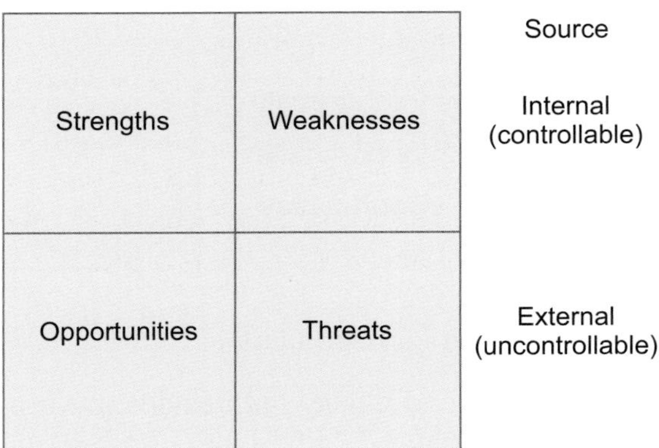

Figure 2.2 SWOT analysis (Source: Jobber, 2010, p. 46)

An example of what a SWOT analysis might look like in practice can be seen in Box 2.1.

Box 2.1 SWOT Analysis for a medium-sized soft furnishing retailer operating 25 retail stores

Strengths

- Excellent customer service
- Loyal customer base of middle income families
- Clear focus on specialist niche market
- Fast bespoke design services

Weaknesses

- Products are of very good quality but designs are a bit dated

- Lack of marketing expertise
- lack of knowledge of web marketing

Opportunities

- Growing market demand from upmarket customers
- Economic conditions – movement in the housing market is slow so many homeowners are refurbishing

Threats

- Economic conditions – consumers are becoming price sensitive
- Growth opportunities in key markets mean there are more competitors entering the soft furnishing market.

As soon as a SWOT analysis is completed it is important to make use of the information as part of the wider marketing planning process.

Activity 2.4 SWOT and strategy development

Spend about 20 minutes on this activity

Purpose: to examine the use of the SWOT analysis

Task: Study figure 2.3 and then make suggestions of how our medium-sized soft furnishing retailer might:

1 convert weaknesses into strengths

2 match strengths with opportunities

3 convert threats into opportunities.

Feedback

1. Convert weaknesses into strengths

Products are of very good quality but designs are a bit dated – the retailer needs to invest some time and effort into updating designs, which could be achieved by visiting trade exhibitions. The management needs to acknowledge the importance of updating the product ranges.

Lack of marketing expertise – this is a medium sized company so it might be possible to employ a marketing consultant to help develop a coherent marketing plan, which would include the use of web marketing.

2. Match strengths with opportunities

Excellent customer service aligns well with the growing market demand from upmarket customers, so there are good opportunities to develop this market. Investment in increasing the spend of existing customers and also attracting new customers should bring dividends.

Loyal customer base of middle income families aligns with the economic conditions – movement in the housing market is slow so many homeowners are refurbishing. This creates opportunities for the retailer to encourage loyal customers to make repeat orders. A launch for a new designer range of high fashion furnishings could be very successful.

3. Convert threats into opportunities

Growing market demand from upmarket customers is an opportunity to extend the business but the retailer must be aware of competitors trying to enter the market by offering low prices. Introducing a price driven promotion to introduce the new designer range could be used to convert the potential threat from new competitors and also deal with the issue of consumers becoming more price sensitive.

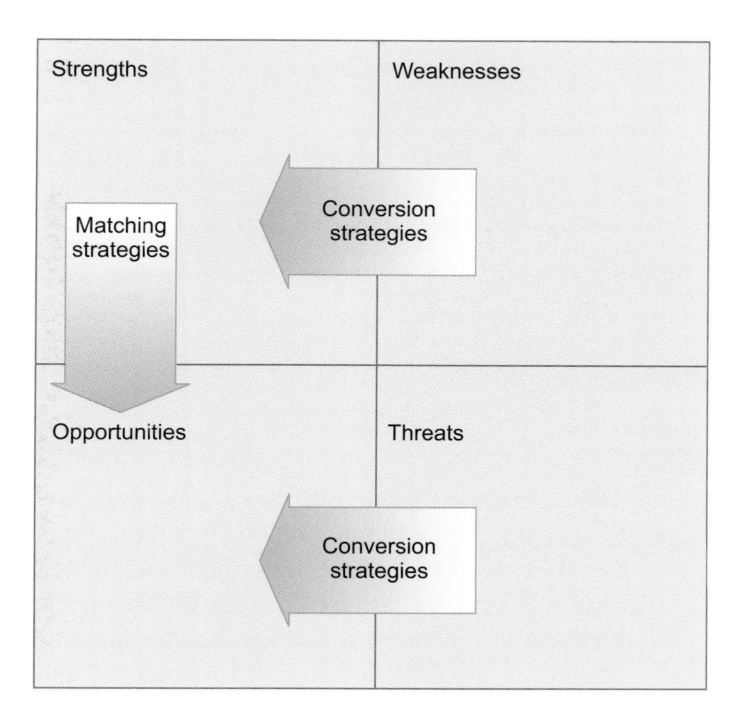

Figure 2.3 SWOT analysis and strategy development (Source: Jobber, 2010, p. 47)

2.5 Marketing objectives

The next stage in the process is to set specific marketing objectives as they provide clear direction. There are two types of marketing objectives: strategic thrust and strategic objectives.

Strategic thrust

Objectives should be set in terms of which products to sell in which markets. This describes the *strategic thrust* of the business, which defines its future direction. The alternatives comprise concentrating on:

- existing products in existing markets (market penetration or expansion)
- new/related products for existing markets (product development)
- existing products in new/related markets (market development)
- new/related products for new/related markets (entry into new markets).

Figure 2.4 shows these options.

		Markets	
		Existing	New/related
Products	Existing	Market penetration or expansion	Market development
	New/related	Product development	Enter new markets

Figure 2.4 Strategic thrust options (Source: Jobber, 2010, p. 48)

Market penetration

Jobber states:

> This strategy is to take the existing product in the existing market and to attempt increased penetration. Existing customers may become more brand loyal (brand-switch less often) and/or new customers in the same market may begin to buy the brand. Other tactics to increase penetration include getting existing customers to use the brand more often (e.g., wash their hair more frequently) and to use a greater quantity when they use it (e.g., two spoonfuls of tea instead of one). The latter tactic would also have the effect of expanding the market.
>
> (Jobber, 2010, p. 48)

One retail product category which has historically relied on market penetration strategies is cereals. Cereals were once widely known as 'breakfast' cereals, but manufacturers and retailers have worked together to encourage consumers to eat 'breakfast' cereals at any time of the day. You may have noticed television adverts for cereals later in the evening; this scheduling serves two key purposes: (1) to encourage you to have an evening snack; (2) to ensure that the particular brand of cereal is in your mind for the morning.

Product development

According to Jobber, pursuing the product development strategy involves:

> ...increasing sales by improving present products or developing new products for current markets ... Product development may take the form of brand extensions (e.g., Anadin Extra, Maximum Strength and Soluble) that provide slightly modified features for target customers.
>
> (Jobber, 2010, pp. 48–9)

Staying with our cereal category, think for a moment about the different types of cereal-related products you might buy.

Eating a cereal bar on the move

Cereal bars are a good example of product developments which are targeted at the same market but encourage us to consume the product in different ways and in different settings, for example, breakfast on the move, midday snack, outdoor convenience food.

Market development

This strategy involves targeting new customers with existing products. When a retailer has a successful product range there may be market growth opportunities in new target markets. This can mean selling to different types of consumers (e.g., older, more affluent, less affluent) but often means moving into different geographic locations.

Now read the material below that explores the Global and international retailing theme for this block.

Global and international retailing

Many European and North American retailers have been attracted to the UK by low operating costs and high-spending consumers. Examples are: the USA lingerie retailer Victoria's Secret and H&M in Sweden. Erling Persson established H&M in 1947 selling women's clothes and this successfully expanded from Sweden into other parts of Europe then to the USA and other parts of the world. The company is now renowned for its fast-fashion items.

Box 2.2 Marketing development at Tesco plc.

Tesco Thailand

Tesco is the UK's most successful supermarket chain and accounts for a staggering £1 of every £8 of consumer spending in British shops. The traditional Tesco supermarket was the large superstore offering large food and non-food (e.g., clothing, consumer electronics goods, petrol, CDs) product ranges. These superstores tend to be on the edge of town, with free parking and facilities that include cafés and petrol stations. They target customers who want big, trolley-based family shopping. This one-stop-shopping experience, backed by a good-quality, value-for-money positioning strategy based on the 'Every Little Helps' strap-line ensured healthy sales and profit growth for many years.

In an effort to continue this growth, Tesco embarked on a market development strategy based on entering a new market segment. This was the convenience shopper who wishes to 'top up' their shopping or replace home essentials such as milk or bread. Two new store formats were created, both small but differing in terms of location. Tesco Metro stores allow convenience shopping in town centres, while Tesco Express stores are usually found at petrol stations, providing drivers and local customers with a convenient place to shop for groceries. Both stores carry the same grocery products, albeit a smaller range, than their superstore counterparts.

Tesco has also pursued market development through moving into new geographical markets with similar products. Tesco has expanded into the USA, China, India, South Korea, Thailand, Hungary, Poland and Turkey as it seeks to compete globally with Wal-Mart. Although overseas expansion has sometimes been met with difficulties – most notably in the USA – Tesco's two-pronged market development strategy of seeking to serve new market segments at home, and moving into new geographical markets abroad has been highly successful in maintaining sales and profits growth.

(Jobber, 2010, p. 49, based on www.imaginerecruitment.com and Singh, 2008)

End of theme 

Entry into new markets

Selling new products into new markets is the most risky marketing objective but in certain circumstances it may be the only option, especially if the company's current market is in decline and a future upturn is unlikely.

Strategic objectives

In addition to strategic thrust objectives, which help retailers determine which markets they are going to enter with which product ranges, there are also specific objectives which can be applied at a product level, for example:

- Build – if a retailer is selling a new product or product range, it will need to build sales in order to grow its share of the market, e.g., Blue ray high-definition DVD player.
- Hold – when grocery retailers enter into promotional price wars they are often attempting to protect (i.e. hold) their market share in a particular product category, e.g., seasonal products such as Christmas fare or chocolates at Easter.
- Harvest – the market share of a particular product is allowed to fall but profit margins are maximised.
- Divest – the product is dropped from the range when it is no longer profitable.

By setting objectives at both levels (strategic and product) a retail marketing planner is answering the question 'where would the business like to be?', which is the fourth of our key planning questions.

2.6 Core strategy

The next stage in the planning process is setting out the core strategy. The marketing objectives set out the focus and then the core strategy identifies how these objectives are going to be achieved. There are three key elements: target markets, competitor targets and competitive advantage.

Target markets

> A central plank of core strategy is the choice of target market(s). Marketing is not about chasing any customer at any price. A decision has to be made regarding those groups of customers (segments) that are attractive to the business and match its supply capabilities.
>
> (Jobber, 2010, pp. 50–1)

Nike Plc developed a special retail experience for its customers – Nike Town stores – in order to enhance the company's brand messages. Nike's target customers are energetic young people around 20–30 years old who are looking for highly functional sportswear which is also fashionable.

Retailers need to understand the target market they wish to serve. This image of Nike's visual merchandising gives definite clues to the type of customer in their target market. The marketing planning process helps marketers to focus on identifying the *right* target market. According to Jobber (2010, p. 51) the choice of *target market* [emphasis added] will emerge as a result of the SWOT analysis and the setting of marketing objectives (strategic thrust). For example, the marketing audit upon which SWOT analysis is based will include market segmentation analysis and, when considering the strategic thrust of the business, decisions regarding which markets to serve must be made. However, if this is defined only in broad terms – for example, 'enter the business personal computer market' – there will be a number of segments (customer groups) of varying attractiveness and a choice has to be made regarding which segments to serve.

At this point, it is important to note that a retailer needs to link the analysis from the audit and the SWOT analysis with the company's resources and capabilities in order to develop a core strategy. Other considerations are the ever-changing needs of the consumer, adapting the marketing mix, and if necessary repositioning the retail offer.

2.7 Competitive advantage

Additionally, retail marketing planners must consider which competitors to target. In some situations, competitors can be weak and poorly equipped to respond to an attack.

The link between target markets and competitor targets is the establishment of a competitive advantage. A *competitive advantage* [emphasis added] is the achievement of superior performance through differentiation to provide superior customer value, or by managing to achieve lowest delivered cost. For major success, businesses need to achieve a clear performance differential over the competition on factors that are important to target customers. The most successful methods are built upon some combination of three advantages.

1 *being better* – superior quality or service (e.g., John Lewis, Waitrose, Harvey Nichols)
2 *being faster* – anticipate or respond to customer needs faster than the competition (e.g., Zara)
3 *being closer* – establishing close long-term relationships with customers (e.g., Tesco with its clubcard and associated targeted promotions).

> Another route to competitive advantage is achieving the lowest relative … cost position of all competitors. Lowest cost can be translated into a competitive advantage through low prices, or by producing standard items at price parity when comparative success may be achieved through higher profit margins than those of competitors.
>
> (Adapted from Jobber, 2010, p. 52)

ASDA/Walmart is a good example of a retailer using the lowest cost position in the marketplace as a source of competitive advantage. Jobber defines competitive advantage thus:

> A competitive advantage is the achievement of superior performance through differentiation to provide superior customer value or by managing to achieve lowest delivered cost. The example of the Apple iPod is an example of a company using product features to convey customer benefits in excess of what the competition is offering. The iPod's small size and its ability to download and store music can, therefore, be regarded as the creation of competitive advantages over the previous market leader in portable music players, the Sony Walkman. Aldi, the German supermarket chain, achieves a competitive advantage by severely controlling costs, allowing it to make profits even though its prices are low, a strategy that is attractive to price-sensitive shoppers … The strategy of using advertising as a tool for competitive advantage is often employed when product benefits are particularly subjective … in nature. Thus the advertising for perfumes such as those produced by Chanel, Givenchy and Yves St Laurent is critical in preserving the exclusive image established by such brands. … Finally, distribution decisions need to be made with the customer in mind, not only in terms of availability but also with respect to service levels, image and customer convenience. The Radisson SAS hotel at Manchester Airport is an example of creating a competitive advantage through customer convenience. It is situated five minutes' walk from the airport terminals, which are reached by covered walkways. Guests at rival hotels have to rely on taxis or transit buses to reach the airport.
>
> (Jobber, 2010, p. 21)

The next stage in the marketing planning process is making decisions about how to use the marketing mix.

2.8 Marketing mix decisions

In Multimedia activities 3 you should have developed a good understanding of the implications of using the marketing mix within retailing. According to Jobber (2010, pp. 20–1), understanding the target customer is key to making good marketing mix decisions. During the marketing planning process, a retailer will identify the market segment it aims to target, so that it knows who its customers are. Once the target market is identified, the marketing management needs to understand how customers react to competitors' offerings and to consider the company's products and services from the customer's perspective. In Session 3, you will see how consumers buy in groups and consider how to apply the marketing mix to influence different members of such groups.

Figure 2.5 shows how the marketing mix is linked to customer needs and requirements and the quote from Jobber that follows expands on this.

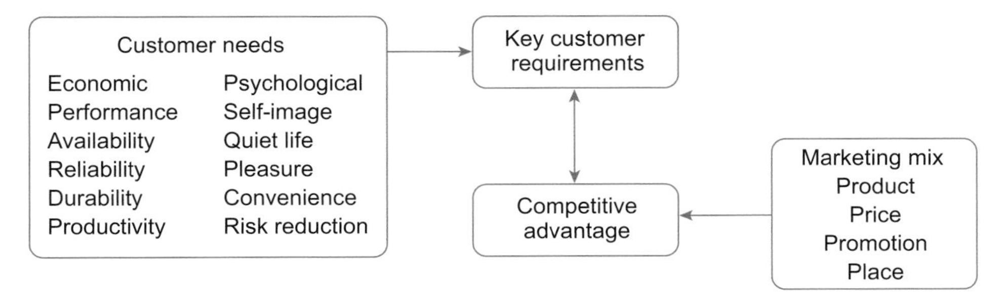

Figure 2.5 Matching the marketing mix to customer needs (Source: Jobber, 2010, Figure 1.8, p. 20)

> The starting point is the realization that customers evaluate products on economic and psychological criteria. Economic criteria include factors such as performance, availability, reliability, durability and productivity gains to be made by using the product. Examples of psychological criteria are self-image, a desire for a quiet life, pleasure, convenience and risk reduction. … The important point at this stage is to note that an analysis of customer choice criteria will reveal a set of key customer requirements that must be met in order to succeed in the marketplace. Meeting or exceeding these requirements better than the competition leads to the creation of a competitive advantage.
>
> (Jobber, 2010, pp. 20–1)

The key point here is that retailers can create competitive advantage based on how they 'blend' the marketing mix.

Activity 2.5 Blending the marketing mix

Spend about 15 minutes on this activity.

Purpose: to reflect on the impact of blending the marketing mix

Task: Study the four pictures of flowers and reflect on how the different colour treatments change the emphasis of the elements of the picture.

Feedback

The black and white and sepia images create a different mood to the second pair of colourful images. You may prefer one of these treatments over and above the rest. Marketers blend the marketing mix to meet the tastes of their target markets in a way that is similar to an artist creating a different effect by the colours used.

The marketing mix is 'blended' in a similar manner to achieve the mix for the target customer, as you can see from the examples below.

ASDA/Walmart blends the mix using:

- product ranges selected to suit the pockets of the target shoppers (everyday quality)
- constantly low prices
- very large supermarket stores
- promotional messages which communicate the 'value for money' position of the brand
- people who are cheerful 'meeters and greeters' at the store entrance
- functional shopping spaces.

Waitrose blends the mix slightly differently using:

- product ranges selected to suit the pockets of the target shoppers (high-quality produce and luxury food brands)
- high prices
- medium-sized supermarket stores
- emotional promotional messages, which communicate the long-term service–quality relationships to position the brand
- highly trained customer service staff
- attractive shopping spaces.

There are no right answers when devising a blend for the marketing mix but the important point is that how a retailer uses the mix is a means of developing competitive advantage.

2.9 Evaluating the marketing strategy

Once a retailer has identified a suitable core strategy and made the marketing mix decisions, it is important to test the suitability of the marketing strategy. Table 2.1 shows a list of considerations which should help test the validity of the strategy.

Table 2.1 Evaluating the market strategy

Action	Implications for retail managers
Assess the extent to which the core strategy clearly defines target customers and their needs	Market research and customer information analysis needed in addition to market analysis
Does the intended strategy provide an opportunity to create competitive advantage?	Understanding of structure and nature of competitive market
Are the risks of applying this strategy reasonable?	Analysis of potential impact on the business; in straightforward terms – what if the strategy is very successful or a complete failure? Assessment of the implied risks
Does the retailer have sufficient resources, e.g., financial, staffing, training?	Assessment of resources and capabilities
Is the plan internally consistent both in terms of the marketing objectives and the overall strategy?	Internal evaluation, e.g., if a retailer is following a cost-leadership strategy, then all subsequent plans are likely to be associated with driving operational costs down

(Source: based on Jobber, 2010, Figure 2.6, p. 53)

2.10 Organisation, implementation and control

The final stages of the planning process involve implementation and control. If a marketing plan is going to succeed, a retailer should ensure that the organisation has the required resources and capabilities.

Implementing new marketing plans may require organisational changes and close attention should be paid to the actual implementation process. There are various potential outcomes.

According to Bonoma (1985, p. 12), if an appropriate strategy is accompanied by a good implementation there will be a successful outcome; if not, the plan is likely to fail. He also suggests that if a good strategy is poorly implemented or a bad strategy is well implemented the outcome is more likely to be like a game of roulette – sometimes a positive outcome and other times negative.

Successful implementation of a marketing strategy requires planning and involves getting support from key decision makers in the company, leveraging appropriate resources, and getting commitment from staff throughout the organisation in terms of both individual staff and departments. It is important to develop appropriate internal communication strategies in order to gain support.

Box 2.3 Staff communication

When Eon – Germany's largest utilities company at the time (2001) – took over the UK electricity provider Powergen, there were many implementation changes for both consumers and employees. The directors made a significant investment in internal communications, part of which consisted of a series of 'road show' events using professional actors to communicate to employees across the company. At these events, the actors staged a public debate, which enabled staff to ask questions and explore the potential impact of the changes for employees and customers; an actor in the role of a member of the catering staff was primed with difficult questions in order to stimulate a thorough and wide-ranging debate from the floor.

A final consideration at the implementation stage is how the marketing function fits into the structure of the organisation. Smaller retail companies can rarely afford to have managers with functional specialisms, for example directors of marketing, finance and operations. Even in larger organisations where individuals are given such responsibilities, not all choose to have a marketing director:

> The classic case of a company that scorned the popular concept of marketing was the Bodyshop. Despite being based on many of the essentials of marketing (e.g., clearly differentiated product range, clear consistent positioning, and effective PR), the Bodyshop refused to set up a marketing department. However, the growth of me-too brands led to the need to reappraise the role of marketing through the establishment of a marketing department in 1994
>
> (Hewitt, 1991, in Jobber, 2010, pp. 796–7)

Nevertheless, as companies grow it is more than likely that an organisation marketing structure will develop as the importance of the marketing function is realised.

It is important not to forget or dismiss the final element of the planning process: control.

Activity 2.6 Stages in planning a journey revisited

Spend about 10 minutes on this activity.

Purpose: to reflect on the importance of the concept of control as part of the planning process.

Task: Think back to the journey you planned in Activity 2.2 and now imagine going on that trip. Suggest how you might evaluate whether the trip was a success and suggest some consequences of bad planning which might render your trip unsuccessful.

Feedback

My example journey was a shopping expedition to find a gift for a friend's special birthday celebration.

My goal was not to actually make the purchase but to identify some suitable options as several other friends wished to contribute to the gift.

However, it turned out that I got held up and consequently my browsing time was significantly reduced. This meant I had time to visit only a couple of stores, and the selection of suggested gifts was severely reduced and more expensive than I originally planned as I did not have sufficient time to make a more considered selection. My friends were disappointed with my suggestions and so the outcome was that we agreed to put a cash donation in a card instead.

Evaluation:

- Availability of resources, in this case time, was insufficient.
- Assessment of outcomes – the poor solution affected my self-image, the quality of the final gift choice and my personal credibility.

Although this is a hypothetical situation the message should be clear: careful planning and considered, well-resourced implementation should result in better outcomes all round.

2.11 Conclusions

In this study session, we have explored the marketing planning process and identified a number of discrete stages in the planning process that a retailer should consider when developing a marketing plan. We considered the elements which make up the marketing audit and SWOT analysis and how the planning process links into setting marketing objectives and planning to use the marketing mix.

In the next study session you will learn more about consumer behaviour and its impact on marketing planning.

Learning outcomes

When you have completed all the study elements for this session, you should be able to:

- describe the stages in the marketing planning process
- identify and consider issues, which can be addressed by marketing planning
- draw on and apply marketing theories to help solve management problems and issues
- use your own experiences to learn about retail marketing.

In addition you should have developed your learning by completing the activities and study materials.

Session 3 Consumer behaviour

This session will focus on consumer behaviour by looking at the marketing implications of the stages in the buying process, and the variables that affect purchasing decisions from both rational and emotional perspectives. This builds on the work you have already done in Block 2, where you considered consumers' attitudes and experiences in relation to managing service encounters.

By the end of the session, you should have a clear understanding of the importance of the consumer decision making process to marketing and retail branding, as well as an understanding of why individuals behave differently when selecting their favourite brands.

Extreme customer service

For retail marketers to encourage customers to visit and return to their stores, they need to understand consumers and how their stores deliver benefits to each individual. The cartoon 'Extreme customer service' illustrates how easy it is to set out with good intentions but to get it completely wrong.

Extreme customer service

Market research is the process of gathering data using various techniques, e.g., a questionnaire, an interview or an online survey, to produce information about the current situation in a given market. It may also be useful for collecting information about customer buying habits through loyalty cards.

A way to get to know customers better is to answer the following questions:

1 Who is important in the buying decision?

2 How do they buy?

3 What are their choice criteria?

4 Where do they buy?

5 When do the buy?

Increasingly, retailers find answers to these important questions using online and offline market research techniques.

Let's look at the implications of these questions.

3.1 Who is important in the buying decision?

This may seem an obvious question but, whilst you may be the only person involved when you buy a bottled drink or a snack bar, when you buy an item like, say, a new pair of training shoes, a new car or furniture for your home, it is very likely that there are other people involved in the buying decision.

According to Blackwell et al. (2005), there are five separate roles which are performed in what they call a *buying centre*:

1 the *initiator*, who starts the buying process

2 the *influencer*, who aims to persuade others in the buying centre to behave in a particular way

3 the *decider*, who makes the final purchase decision; this person has the power and/or authority within the group to take this action

4 the *buyer*, who conducts the actual buying transaction

5 the *user*, who actually uses the product.

Please be aware that 'buying centre' can be used in business-to-business buying as well as consumer buying. Throughout this session, however, the term refers to a consumer buying.

A cartoon by Haselden from 1912 (Source: www.cartoon.ac.uk)

Haselden's (1912) stereotype cartoon 'A study on prices' depicts how the make-up of the buying group can affect the purchase decision. In the first image the woman in the large hat is shopping alone and is considering relatively low-priced hats (the prices are all under £2). In the second image, when she is accompanied by her husband, the prices of the hats are significantly more. (GNS stands for guineas and a guinea was a British coin, valued from 1717 onwards at £1.05, which means the lowest priced option is in excess of £14.)

When the woman is shopping alone, we might assume that she takes on the roles of initiator, decider, buyer and user, and the sales assistant acts as the influencer. However, when the woman is accompanied by her husband, the implication is that he takes on the role of decider and buyer, the woman is the initiator and the user, and the sales assistant again acts as the influencer.

This situation gives us some clues about the importance of the make-up of the buying group to the retail marketer: prices can be set at different levels depending on who is doing the deciding and the buying.

Activity 3.1 Buying centre purchasing

Spend about 15 minutes on this activity.

Purpose: to gain understanding of the buying centre model and roles.

Task: Imagine you are going to buy two items, one costing under £5 and one costing over £200. Note your two items and the approximate cost of each one.

Now use Blackwell et al.'s descriptions of the five roles to determine who might influence your purchase decision.

Feedback

My first purchase is two ice creams (approximate cost £3.50).

In this purchase situation, I was the *initiator*. It was a warm sunny day and I was out walking with my son in a Derbyshire village. My son was an *influencer*, as he wanted a soft-scoop ice cream and wanted me to have the same. However, I was the *decider* as I was paying for the ice cream. I chose a speciality strawberry ice cream for myself and my son had his soft scoop. In this case, my son did not influence my decision, as I love strawberry ice cream. I was also the *buyer* as I went into the shop and made the purchase, and also the *user* as I ate the ice cream.

My second purchase is a new computer (approximate cost £800).

In this situation, the make-up of the buying centre is very different. My husband was the *initiator*; he suggested I get a new computer as our existing machine was rather old. Our son was an *influencer*, as he works in computing and has always had a keen interest in the web and computer gaming. I was the *decider* as I was paying for the computer. I was also the *buyer*; I bought the computer online. All three of us are *users* of the computer.

It is important to note that individuals can play more than one role in the buying centre and there can also be more than one individual fulfilling each role.

Why is it important to understand who is doing the buying and who else is involved in the buying centre? If a retailer understands the roles and individuals in a typical buying centre they are better able to tailor the elements of the marketing mix and the promotional mix to suit the needs of the individuals involved. In other words, they have a better chance of getting right the mix of price, product quality, place where the product is sold, and the way in which it is promoted.

As you read in Block 1, shopper demographics are changing. More men are involved in weekly shopping and teenagers play an increasingly important role in electronic purchases such as computers and broadband connections. Therefore, it is very important for retailers to understand the buying centre in order to determine the needs of the target market.

3.2 How do people buy and what choice criteria do they use?

There is a widely recognised process called the consumer decision making process, which explains the stages an individual will pass through when making a buying decision.

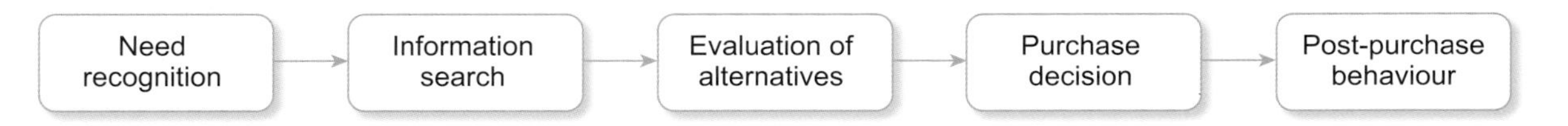

Figure 3.1 Stages in the buying decision process (Source: Blackwell, Miniard and Engel, 2005).

Each of the stages in the process illustrated in Figure 3.1 has important marketing implications.

Need recognition

Need recognition (also referred to as problem awareness) in its most basic form is a functional requirement: for example, you are thirsty, your car is running low on petrol, there is no food in your store cupboard. In these cases you will go out and buy replacement goods. Each of these is an example of *routine depletion*. The purchase solution is straightforward: replace the product that has been consumed. There are other situations where the decision is more complex or unpredictable: for example, losing your mobile phone or the washing machine breaking down.

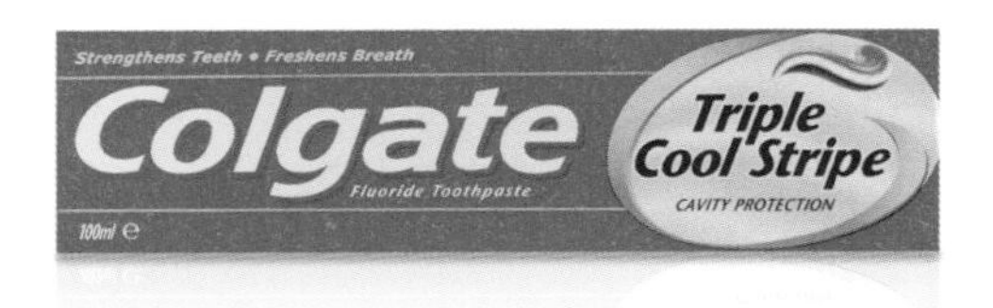

From knowledge of their customers' need recognition, retail marketing managers are aware of the trigger for the buying situation and can identify how to offer the customer a solution. For example, if you are selling washing machines and a customer is replacing a broken machine, it is important that there is not a long lead-time from purchase to order delivery.

Many product manufacturers use need recognition to stimulate sales: for example, shampoos which control dandruff, toothpaste which stops tooth decay, yoghurts which take care of the stomach.

Information search

Buyers engage in information searching according to the importance of the purchase. In Activity 3.1 my ice cream purchase was a very limited search as there were only two shops to choose from and only one had the ice cream I wanted. However, for the computer purchase there were many alternatives. So in order to evaluate which was the best option we gathered information on available computers and retail suppliers.

According to Jobber (2010, p.113), the objective of information searching is to create an *awareness set* (the number of different product brands that might offer a solution). It is important to note that the internet is playing an increasingly important role in the consumer decision making process as individuals go online to search for product information. In response to this change in consumer behaviour, price comparison websites have emerged selling product knowledge and pricing information, for example, Kelkoo.co.uk, which compares products in most retail categories.

Reflection

Has your shopping behaviour changed as a result of the emergence of the internet as a shopping and information channel? If so, how has it changed?

Evaluation of alternatives

Once the searching is over, it is time to reduce the choices. The individual intending to make a purchase will reduce the *awareness set* to an *evoked set*, which is a set of brands that they seriously consider buying. Consumers use different criteria to reduce the product choice. It is important for the retail marketing manager to understand the key criteria consumers use at this stage if their company or product is to be in the evoked set from which the final purchase item will be chosen. There are many criteria which can affect consumer choice:

- *technical* criteria, e.g., reliability, performance, delivery, taste
- *economic* criteria, e.g., price, value for money, running costs
- *social* criteria, e.g., status, social belonging, fashion
- *personal* criteria, e.g., self-image, ethics, emotions (Jobber, 2010, pp. 114, 118).

The number, importance and influence of choice criteria are likely to depend on the nature of the purchase and the consumer's level of involvement.

Now read 'Evaluation of alternatives and the purchase'.

Box 3.1 Evaluation of alternatives and the purchase (Jobber (2010) p. 114).

A key determinant of the extent to which consumers evaluate a brand is their level of *involvement*. Involvement is the degree of perceived relevance and personal importance accompanying the brand choice.[1] When a purchase is highly involving, the consumer is more likely to carry out extensive evaluation. High-involvement purchases are likely to include those incurring high expenditure or personal risk, such as a car or home buying. [In other words the risk of making the *wrong* decision is also factored into the buying process.] In contrast, low-involvement situations are characterized by simple evaluations about purchases. Consumers use simple choice tactics to reduce time and effort rather than maximize the consequences of the purchase.[2] For example, when purchasing baked beans or breakfast cereal, consumers are likely to make quick choices rather than agonize over the decision.

This distinction between high- and low-involvement situations implies different evaluative processes. For high-involvement purchases the Fishbein and Ajzen theory of reasoned action[3] has proven robust in predicting purchase behaviour,[4] while in low-involvement situations work by Ehrenberg and Goodhart has shown how simple evaluation and decision-making can be.[5] Each of these models will now be examined.

Fishbein and Ajzen model:

This model suggests that an attitude towards a brand is based upon a set of beliefs about the brand's attributes (e.g., value for money, durability). Each attribute is weighted by how good or bad the consumer believes the attribute is likely to be. Those attributes that are weighted highly will have a large influence in the formation of attitude (e.g., if a consumer believes that Brand X will last longer than Brand Y this belief will shape the longer-term attitude towards the brand). Attitude is the degree to which someone likes or dislikes the brand overall. The link between personal beliefs and attitudes is shown in Figure 3.2a.

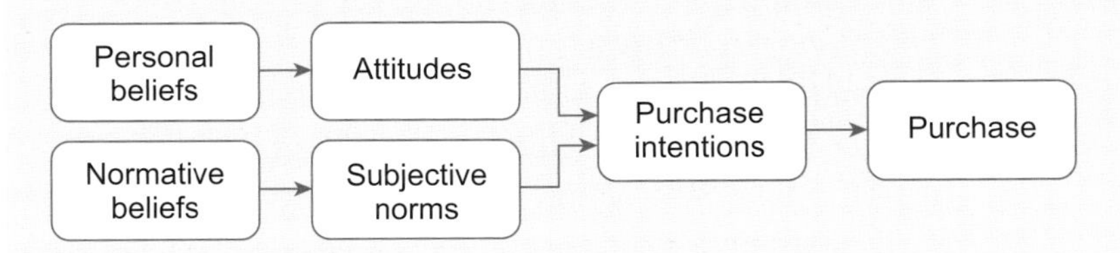

Figure 3.2a Evaluation and purchase model: High involvement: the Fishbein and Ajzen model of reasoned action

However, evaluation of a brand is not limited to personal beliefs about the consequences of buying a brand. Outside influences also play a part. Individuals will thus evaluate the extent to which *important others* believe that they should or should not buy the brand. These beliefs may conflict with their personal beliefs. People may personally believe that buying a sports car may have positive consequences (providing fun driving, being more attractive to other people) but refrain from doing so if they believe that important others (e.g., parents, boss) would disapprove of the purchase. This collection of *normative beliefs* forms an overall evaluation of the degree to which these outside influences approve or disapprove of the purchase (*subjective norms*). The link between normative beliefs and subjective norms is shown in Figure 3.2a. This clearly is a *theory of reasoned action*. Consumers are highly involved in the purchase to the extent that they evaluate the consequences of the purchase *and* what others will think about it. Only after these considerations have taken place does purchase intention and the ultimate purchase result.

The Fishbein and Ajzen model can be illustrated by using the smartphone. Having conducted the search for information, the evoked set comprises an iPhone and BlackBerry. The buyer believes that buying an iPhone would result in a significant cost saving and that both models are virtually identical on other attributes (e.g., reliability, design and speed). Cost savings are very important to this person and so is rated as a very good attribute to possess. The buyer, therefore, has a more favourable attitude towards the iPhone. Furthermore, a close friend, whose opinion the buyer regards as important, owns an iPhone, rates it highly and would strongly approve of such a purchase. Therefore, subjective norms also favour the iPhone. This leads to a purchase intention to buy the iPhone and subsequently its purchase. If the friend was perceived to disapprove of the iPhone purchase, the decision would depend on the relative strengths of the attitude and subjective norm components. When attitudes outweigh subjective norms, the iPhone would be purchased and, for the opposite case, the BlackBerry would be chosen.

Ehrenberg and Goodhart model:

In low-involvement situations the amount of information processing implicit in the earlier model may not be worthwhile or sensible. A typical low-involvement situation is the *repeat purchase* of fast-moving consumer goods (FMCGs, e.g., cereals and milk). The work of Ehrenberg and Goodhart suggests that a very simple process may explain purchase behaviour (see Fig. 3.2b). According to this model, awareness precedes trial, which, if satisfactory, leads to repeat purchase. This is an example of a behavioural model of consumer behaviour: the behaviour becomes *habitual* with little conscious thought or formation of attitudes preceding behaviour. The limited importance of the purchase simply does not warrant the reasoned evaluation of alternatives implied in the Fishbein and Ajzen model. The notion of low involvement suggests that awareness precedes behaviour and behaviour precedes attitude. In this situation the consumer does not actively seek information but is a passive recipient. Furthermore, since the decision is not inherently involving, the consumer is likely to search for a satisfactory solution rather than the best one.[6] Consequently any of several brands that lie in the evoked set may be considered adequate.

Figure 3.2b Evaluation and purchase model: Low involvement: the Ehrenberg and Goodhart repeat purchase model

Distinguishing between high- and low-involvement situations

The distinction between these two purchasing situations is important because the variations in how consumers evaluate products and brands lead to contrasting marketing implications. The complex evaluation outlined in the high-involvement situation suggests that marketing managers need to provide a good deal of information about the positive consequences of buying. Messages with *high information content* would enhance knowledge about the brand; because the consumer is actively seeking information, high levels of repetition are not needed.[7] Print media and websites may be appropriate in the high-involvement case since they allow detailed and repeated scrutiny of information. Typically, new car advertisements often provide information about the comfort, reliability and performance of the model, and also appeal to status considerations. All of these appeals may influence the consumer's beliefs about the consequences of buying the model.

Differential advantage is when there is a clear difference between competing products or companies in terms of the criteria which are important and inform consumers' choice.

The salesforce also has an important role to play in the high-involvement situation by ensuring that the customer is aware of the important attributes of the product and correctly evaluates their consequences. For example, if the *differential advantage* of a particular model of a car is fuel economy the salesperson would raise fuel economy as a salient product attribute and explain the cost benefits of buying that model vis-à-vis the competition.

For low-involvement situations, as we have seen, the evaluation of alternatives is much more rudimentary, and attitude change is likely to follow purchase. In this case, attempting to gain *top-of-mind awareness* through advertising and providing positive *reinforcement* (e.g., through sales promotion) to gain trial may be more important than providing masses of information about the consequences of buying the brand. Furthermore, as this is of little interest, the consumer is not actively seeking information but is a passive receiver. Consequently advertising messages should be *short* with a small number of key points but with *high repetition* to enhance learning.[8] Television may be the best medium since it allows passive reception to messages while the medium actively transmits them. Also, it is ideal for the transmission of short, highly repetitive messages. Much soap powder advertising follows this format.[9]

Marketers must be aware of the role of emotion in consumer evaluation of alternatives. A major source of high emotion is when a product is high in symbolic meaning. Consumers believe that the product helps them to construct and maintain their self-concept and sense of identity. Furthermore, ownership of the product will help them communicate the desired image to other people.[10] Instead, consumers consult their feelings for information about a decision: 'How do I feel about it?' Consequently, many marketers attempt to create a feeling of warmth about their brands. The mere exposure to a brand name over time, and the use of humour in advertisements, can create such feelings.

Impulse buying is another area that can be associated with emotions. Consumers have described a compelling feeling that was 'thrilling', 'wild', 'a tingling sensation', 'a surge of energy', and 'like turning up the volume'.[11]

Numbered references

1 Blackwell, Miniard and Engel (2005) op. cit.

2 Elliott, R. and E. Hamilton (1991) Consumer Choice Tactics and Leisure Activities, *International Journal of Advertising* 10, 325-32.

3 Ajzen, I. and M. Fishbein (1980) *Understanding Attitudes and Predicting Social Behaviour*, Englewood Cliffs, NJ: Prentice-Hall.

4 See e.g., Budd, R.J. and C.P. Spencer (1984) Predicting Undergraduates' Intentions to Drink, *Journal of Studies on Alcohol* 45(2), 179-83; Farley, J., D. Lehman and M. Ryan (1981) Generalizing from 'Imperfect' Replication, *Journal of Business* 54 (4), 597-610; Shrimp, T. and A. Kavas (1984) The Theory of Reasoned Action Applied to Coupon Usage, *Journal of Consumer Research* 11, 795-809.

5 Ehrenberg, A.S.C. and G.J. Goodhart (1980) *How Advertising Works*, J. Walter Thompson/ MRCA.

6 Wright, P.L. (1974) The Choice of a Choice Strategy: Simplifying vs Optimizing, Faculty Working Paper no. 163, Champaign, I11: Department of Business Administration, University of Illinois.

7 Rothschild, M.L. (1978) Advertising Strategies for High and Low Involvement Situations, *American Marketing Association Educator's Proceedings*, Chicago, 150-62.

8 Rothschild (1978) op.cit.

9 For a discussion of the role of involvement in package labelling see Davies, M.A.P. and L.T. Wright (1994) The Importance of Labelling Examined in Food Marketing, *European Journal of Marketing* 28(2), 57–67.

10 Elliott, R. (1997) Understanding Buyers: Implications for Selling, in D. Jobber (ed.) *The CIM Handbook of Selling and Sales Strategy*, Oxford: Butterworth-Heinemann.

11 See Elliott, R. (1998) A Model of Emotion-Driven Choice, *Journal of Marketing Management* 14, 95–108; Rook, D. (1987) The Buying Impulse, *Journal of Consumer Research* 14(1), 89–99.

(Adapted from Jobber, 2010, pp. 114–16)

Activity 3.2 The importance of involvement in consumer decision making

Spend about 30 minutes on this activity.

Purpose: to extend your understanding of how consumers evaluate purchase options.

Task: Complete the following questions:

(a) Choose an item you might like to buy, for example, a pair of training shoes, a bottle of perfume, a box of chocolates. Then build up a list of all of the product brands you can find which might provide a purchase solution. This will give you the awareness set.

(b) Now make a list of the key choice criteria you would use to reduce the list to an evoked set of product options.

(c) Now eliminate the products which do not meet your criteria.

(d) Think about whether this would be a high- or low-involvement purchase.

Feedback

My example is when I recently bought a new car.

(a) It is important to note that there is a total set of product brands, which includes *all* car manufacturers. However, the awareness set is the range of brands which I perceive may offer a possible solution to my problem. My awareness set for my car purchase included the following companies:

Alfa Romeo
Audi
BMW
Citroen
Fiat
Ford
Honda
Hyundai
Jaguar
Land Rover
Lotus
Mazda
MG (Rover)
Mini (BMW)
Mitsubishi
Nissan
Peugeot
Proton
Renault
Seat
Skoda
Suzuki
Toyota
Vauxhall
Volkswagen
Volvo

(b) My key choice criteria for selecting a new car were as follows.

Technical:

design of car, e.g., 2-door; 4-door, hatchback

reliability

fuel efficiency

style/looks

after-sales service.

Economic:

cost of purchase

running costs

taxation.

(c) By using these criteria, it was relatively easy to reduce the length of the list. My budget was £12,000 for the purchase of a new car, so I began by using cost of purchase. This reduced the list to the following manufacturers, based on dealers' prices at the time of writing (2010):

Citroen

Fiat

Ford

Kia

Nissan

Peugeot

Renault

Seat

Skoda

Toyota

Vauxhall.

I then reduced the list again using style/looks and the other main choice criteria of the models available within my budget. This created my evoked set – the manufacturers which I intended to consider before making the purchase. The list included:

Fiat

Nissan

Peugeot

Renault

Seat

Skoda.

I then went to my local dealers to test-drive suitable makes and models before making my choice. Finally, I chose a Skoda Fabia.

(d) For me, this car purchase was a high involvement purchase influenced by technical and economic criteria. Often car buyers use personal and social choice criteria. Manufacturers of new cars focus on the emotional side of the buying process when producing advertising messages.

Purchase decision and post-purchase behaviour

After evaluating the alternatives, the consumer can decide which particular item to buy. At this stage, the retailer needs to be ready to fulfil the consumer requests. Once the purchase is made, there is an important period when the consumer assesses whether they have made the right choice. If they have concerns, this experience is called '*post-purchase dissonance*' (Jobber, 2010, p. 116). It is important to allay any concerns because otherwise the customer may return the product to the store. More importantly, a retailer should endeavour to deliver customer satisfaction, which means offering good after-sales care to ensure that the customer does not reject the product and to reinforce the belief that they made the 'right' choice in the first place. Don't forget that customer satisfaction is at the heart of successful marketing.

3.3 Influences on consumers' purchasing

The choice of where to buy is critically important to retailers. Before considering store choice let's consider the influence of the type of need and/ or buying problem that the consumer is trying to satisfy or solve.

According to Jobber (2010, p. 121), there are three buying situations:

1 *Extended problem solving*. The highly involved consumer requires a great deal of product information, makes a detailed examination of alternatives and applies many choice criteria. Examples are buying a car, a computer, or a valuable piece of jewellery.
2 *Limited problem solving*. The consumer has some experience of the product they are about to buy and may do a limited evaluation such as checking prices when making certain purchases. Retail marketing techniques (discussed in detail in Multimedia activities 3) are used to influence brand switching in this type of problem solving.
3 *Habitual problem solving*. The consumer is making repeat purchases, there is very little evaluation of alternatives, the same products are bought as on previous occasions. Think about your weekly food shopping. How often to you repeatedly buy the same type of products? I've been buying 415g tins of Heinz baked beans for the last 30 years and would never consider an alternative. For me, 'Beanz meanz Heinz' (this product's advertising slogan worked on me at a very young age). This brings me to the importance of personal influences.

In addition, there are personal and social influences which affect where and when consumers make their purchases.

Personal influences

We are all different. As a result we choose to buy different types of product and service. We looked at behaviour and motivations from the retailer's perspective in Block 2, whilst studying customer service. Here we are adding further influences that affect consumer behaviour. According to Jobber (2010), there are six influences on consumer behaviour:

1 **Information processing** – the processes involved in how we receive, store and interpret information. Information processing is of great interest as it helps marketers understand how consumers make purchasing choices. Many market research studies aim to discover more about consumers' perceptions but recent technological developments have facilitated the use of magnetic resonance image (MRI) scanning to gain more scientifically based insight into how consumers' brains actually process information. This high-tech marketing approach is referred to as 'neuro-marketing'.
2 **Motivation** – our needs and goals are what drives us to solve problems and achieve goals. At the most basic level are *physical* motivations: survival (e.g., to be able to satisfy our hunger), and safety (e.g., protection from the unexpected). There are also *socially driven* motivations: belonging and love (e.g., the need to be accepted by those who are close to you, and esteem and status within your social reference groups). The final level of motivation is the desire for *self-fulfilment* – in other words achieving what you are capable of for your own sake (Maslow, 1954, pp. 80–106). Many of us study educational and vocational courses for this very reason.
3 **Beliefs and attitudes** – how what we believe to be *true* shapes our views and subsequent behaviour. Beliefs are very important and are often used by marketers to encourage changes in behaviour. It is many shoppers' belief that the supermarket chain Sainsbury's sells good-quality but expensive groceries. During the 2008–09 global economic recession, Sainsbury's set about dispelling this belief about high cost with a high-profile television advertising campaign which aimed to encourage more people to consider Sainsbury's as a viable option for their grocery shopping.
4 **Personality** – the inner psychological characteristics of individuals which shape their responses to particular situations (Kassarjian, 1971). Personality is widely used, especially in branding, to create links between buyers and sellers.
5 **Lifestyle** – the ways we live our lives. According to Jobber (2010, p. 129), 'lifestyle refers to the pattern of living as expressed in a person's activities, interests and opinions'. In Block 2, we looked at the different shopper types – for example, apathetic, enthusiasts, bargain seekers – which retailers have used to develop customer service programmes. Again, market research is widely used to identify discrete patterns of shopper behaviour. Lifestyles have become increasingly important, particularly in the food and drink sector where this kind of personalisation has become increasingly popular, with consumers' individual nutritional needs, aspirations and preferences bolstered by the food and drink products they buy (Pilcher, 2008).
6 **Life-cycle and age** – the stage of life a consumer has reached. Purchasing behaviour changes according to a person's life situation. For example, young and living at home with parents, young married parents, middle aged and divorced with no children, retired and married with no children living at home, retired and living on one's own. The stage in the

life-cycle is important to retailers as it affects the products people require, their disposable income and the amount they are prepared to spend. Age is also a useful discriminator as it helps to predict individual tastes.

It is very important for marketers to understand not only the buying situation but also the personal influences which affect consumer behaviour. Market-orientated retailers such as Sainsbury's invest in finding out about their customers and their personal influences in order to tailor the marketing mix to meet consumers' requirements.

Store choice

McGoldrick (2002, pp. 103–4) suggests that store choice is linked to the type of buying situation. Consumers can be creatures of habit and in this situation the retailer should aim to ensure that the shopping experience is within the customers' expectations in terms of say, the number of sales staff, organisation of the store and product availability. Failure to meet expectations can kick-start the customer into re-evaluating where to shop.

According to Nielsen (2008), 'five in six shoppers claim good value is more important than range, location, convenience and environmental friendliness'. This regular study of over 25,000 internet users around the world found that over 85 per cent of the world's consumers ranked good value for money as the most important consideration when selecting a grocery store. It is important to note that both location and convenience are also influences.

Activity 3.3 Reasons for choosing where to shop

Spend about 15 minutes on this activity.

Purpose: to identify attributes of a store which might affect consumer choice of where to shop.

Task: Make a list of the attributes you use when selecting where to do your grocery shopping.

Feedback

Possible attributes which affect store choice include:

- value for money
- convenient location
- ease of parking
- low prices
- range of products available
- cleanliness and attractiveness of the store
- quality of own-label products
- quality of fresh produce
- availability of specialist and high-quality products
- in-store promotions
- helpfulness of the staff
- proximity to where you live

- availability of parking space
- store opening hours
- other facilities such as a petrol station or coffee shop
- recreational facilities
- situation of the store in relation to other shops.

(Based on McGoldrick, 2002, p. 94)

The attributes of a store will affect the behaviour of consumers. Many retailers conduct extensive research in order to determine how to shape their offer to meet the needs of their customers, and in doing so create distinctive brands.

3.4 Conclusions

In retail marketing it is important to understand the nuances of consumer behaviour in order to develop successful marketing campaigns. In this session we have built on your understanding of consumer behaviour from Blocks 1 and 2 by focusing on the actual buying process and the elements of the consumer decision making process which affect how, what, where and when consumers choose to buy. We have also considered the importance of buying centres and how such groups have implications for marketing.

The final session in this book will explore the concept of branding.

Learning outcomes

When you have completed all the study elements for this session, you should be able to:

- describe the consumer buying process
- identify the influences which affect how consumers buy
- discuss the implications of consumer behaviour on retail marketing and planning
- use your own experiences to learn about consumer behaviour.

Session 4 Retail brands

Well-known brands tend to dominate the markets they operate in and the importance of strong brands means that brand building has become an important marketing activity. Figure 4.1 shows some of the best-known brands in the UK.

Figure 4.1 UK brands

> Branding is the process by which companies distinguish their product offerings from the competition, by developing a distinctive name, packaging and design a brand is created. Some brands are supported by logos – for example, the Nike Swoosh and the prancing horse of Ferrari. By developing a distinctive individual identity, branding permits customers to develop associations with the brand (e.g., prestige, economy) and eases the purchase decision.
>
> (DeChertoney, 1991, in Jobber, 2010 p. 303)

> Retail branding has developed to such an extent that today retailers are perceived as being brands themselves rather than distributors of manufacturer brands. Many retailers have developed such a strong consumer franchise that customers are more loyal to the retailer than to the manufacturer's brand. This shift is mainly due to extensive development of *own brands* [emphasis added] and a more marketing-orientated approach to retailing. Retailers have been rewarded for their focus on customer needs and aspirations by increased levels of trust from customers.
>
> (Varley and Rafiq, 2004, p. 204)

From these quotes you can see how important it is to learn about retail branding strategies.

4.1 What is a brand?

A brand is the core product augmented by additional distinctive features which add value and deliver specific benefits to its users and there are various types of brands, which we will discuss later in this section e.g., manufacturer brands and own-label brands. Additionally, retailers position themselves as brands. For retailers, building a strong brand is important as it adds to the value of the company, influences consumer behaviour, can act as a barrier to competition and ultimately lead to high profits. You might have heard or read about the term *brand equity*. Brand equity is a measure of the power and importance of a brand in the marketplace which is based on the value attributed to a brand by its customers and its assets e.g., patents, channel relationships.

Think back to Activity 3.2 which explored how we use different choice criteria depending on the importance of the purchase and the level of involvement. The choice criteria we use to make buying decisions align with the brand proposition; in other words the offer the brand makes if we buy a particular product. Take the example of a pair of boots in this image.

The boots are the core product but there are some additional features which can augment the product to produce a brand:

- The quality and design – these boots are designed as walking boots, which implies that the materials used will be highly durable and the boots are designed to maximise comfort on a long walk.
- If the boots were a well-known manufacturer brand there could be additional guarantees and service offers, which augment the original product.

Successful brands are built by providing quality products which deliver the perceived benefits customers expect. A brand can establish a clear differential advantage over its competitors by creating a unique position in the marketplace and in the minds of consumers. The strength of a brand's position in the market is based on its domain, heritage, values, assets, personality and reflection (Jobber, 2010, pp. 314–15). Table 4.1 explains these ideas, using Dr Marten boots as an example.

Table 4.1 The components of a brand's position in the marketplace

Dr Martens brand	Definition
Brand domain	The target market was originally individuals working in manual trades but this extended to include young people between 13 and 25 years old, particularly tribal social groups: skinheads, punks, rockers. The brand also has celebrity buyers.
Brand heritage	The name of the brand comes from its originator, Dr Klaus Marten, who designed the boot whilst recuperating from an injury and found that his army boots were uncomfortable. He designed improvements to the basic boots and added air-filled soles. The story of the brand has developed from the initial design through to today and now has over 50 years of heritage story to tell.
Brand values	The core values and characteristics of the brand are based on high-performance, fashionable, comfortable boots.
Brand assets	The brand has a distinctive brand logo, which distinguishes it from other brands. The boots are very hard wearing and offer a guarantee for the life of the product. The longevity of the brand becomes an asset.
Brand personality	The boots are iconic although they mean different things to different people; they are characterised by freedom and individuality.
Brand reflection	The brand reflection is how individuals perceive themselves as a result of wearing the brand. I had a white pair of DMs which I wore when I first became a university lecturer. My DMs represented freedom and individuality especially when I painted them blue!

Dr Martens sells its distinctive footwear through its own outlets, online and in footwear stores throughout the world. The distinctive features of the brand have enabled the company to create and differentiate a unique brand in the highly competitive footwear sector.

4.2 Growth of retailer own-label brands

Sales of retailer own-label brands have increased substantially over the past few decades:

> The growth of retailer brands, variously known as own brands, own labels, private labels, and store brands has paralleled the growth of multiples, especially in the grocery sector. It was in the 1960s that the major multiple retailers began to realize that they could increase their margins significantly if they did not have to pay for manufacturers' branding overheads. The substantial costs associated with the task of branding mean that branded products are unable to compete on a level price basis with own-brand lines.
>
> (Varley and Rafiq, 2004, p. 205)

Another reason for the growth of own brands was the existence of different customer segments in the marketplace, some of whom were very price conscious and others who were not. This meant that manufacturers could make products for supermarkets without affecting sales unduly.

Shoppers can make significant savings if they choose own brands. For example, (at the time of writing, 2010) a 100g jar of Nescafé Gold blend instant coffee costs £2.05, whereas leading supermarket own-label brands of coffee of similar quality and quantity are available at much lower prices: Tesco Gold £1.38, ASDA Gold £1.38 and Sainsbury's Gold £1.39.

> Retailer brands are important in the grocery sector of the UK retail industry as they account for a significant proportion of sales. Indeed the contribution from own brands has been increasing rapidly during the last twenty years. In fact, commentators suggest that retailer own brands account for 47 per cent of the market.
>
> (Taylor, 2007 p. 2).

Now read the following article – 'Never mind the sizzle ... where's the sausage?'

Never mind the sizzle ... where's the sausage?

In the 1950s hard-nosed salesmen in the US were exhorted to 'sell the sizzle, not the steak'. That message was taken up for decades by advertising and marketing people in recognition of the power of emotional appeal. But the pendulum has swung too far: too much sizzle, not enough steak (or sausage in the UK version). Brand marketing is about balance and that balance has been displaced.

Retail own-label share of UK grocery sales in 1981 was 22%. Today it is 47%. If the trend continues, manufacturer brands risk becoming a supporting actor, not the star of the show. And it's not just a UK issue. We can see the same threat of retail own-labels in other European markets such as Holland and Germany.

Just in case there was any doubt about the intentions of your friendly retail partner, Asda's marketing director spelt it out last year in black and white. He stunned into silence a group of top marketing directors who'd invited him to talk at their conference by saying: 'My job is to "undo" the marketing of brands and drive consumers to own-label alternatives. Our products are not only more profitable, but also of superior quality.'

One explanation for this mess is in the last part of this quote. Many brands have taken their eye off the product ball, seduced by the dual sirens of 'sizzle' and 'stretch'. Sizzle refers to an obsession with the emotional side of branding; and by focusing on this emotional side at the expense of product, or 'sausage', many brands have fallen into the trap of over-stretching into markets where they don't really belong.

This focus on sizzle and stretch at the expense of substance is personified in my new book *Where's the Sausage?* by Hugo Gaines, the marketing director of an imaginary company called Simpson's Sausages. And although Hugo's cringeworthy cock-ups are fictional, he represents a side of marketing that is very real. And very dangerous.

The obsession with sizzle

Many of us in marketing are seeking salvation in the emotional side of branding, to do with values, personality and tone-of-voice. According to the gurus of emotional branding, it is no longer enough to be liked. Your brand needs to become what Hugo calls a 'Hugbrand™', which is loved, not just liked. And the key to creating this emotional bond is through emotional communication.

In lifestyle categories such as fashion and fragrances, emotional sizzle is rightly centre stage, with products playing a secondary, supporting role. New fragrance creation often starts with the name and 'the big picture' visual to use in communication, with the fragrance itself following after.

However, the problems start when marketing teams working on pet food and pasta sauce try to adopt the same lifestyle branding strategies. This is especially dangerous in cases where the product they are selling is identical or even inferior to retailer own-brand competition. We end up with the surreal situation explained to me by a marketing manager of one of the UK's leading laundry cleaning brands. I asked why his brand was 30% more expensive than the retail own-label equivalent. His response? 'We advertise on TV.' When I asked why the brand was advertised on TV his answer was 'To support our premium price.'

Over-stretching the marque

A dangerous side-effect of the focus on emotional sizzle is over-stretching. Climbing a 'ladder' up from a functional, product-based level to the rarefied heights of emotional branding gives the (illusory) freedom to stretch into pretty much any category that takes our fancy. Having a decent product becomes secondary, as long as there is some emotional linkage. Many of the resulting brand extensions are merely 'brand ego trips', lacking any competitive added value.

This thinking led to *Cosmopolitan* deciding it was no longer a magazine. It defined itself as a lifestyle brand that empowered women to be more confident and successful, launching *Cosmopolitan* low-fat yoghurt to compete with Danone.

Gillette decided it was not a shaving brand, it was a 'male grooming brand', and launched into a head-on, bloody battle with Unilever in the deodorant market. And, coming the other way, Unilever's Lynx body spray invested heavily in launching a shaving range. Lynx shaving and *Cosmopolitan* yoghurt ended up in the overcrowded extension graveyard, where over half of all brand extensions go to die. Gillette struggles in deodorants to get anyway near the leading share it has in the shaver market, (though it may have more luck now it's part of P&G).

And while brands have been busy climbing emotional ladders and stretching into new markets, the retail own-label has been busy on product innovation. And they're no longer content with producing low-priced rip-offs of brands; they're leading the way in many categories, creating premium-priced, added-value offerings. Sainsbury's Taste the Difference is now a £450 million brand in its own right, and in some cases higher priced than the manufacturer brands.

Marketing based on substance, not spin

There is an alternative road, although it may not be as glamorous or trendy. Nor is it exactly revolutionary. But it has the potential to add more value for consumers and shareholders alike, by re-focusing brands on substance, not spin.

1 (Re)discovering product passion

The first step is the most fundamental, and perhaps the hardest. For many it requires a change in culture and mindset. It requires us to stop focusing on creating an emotional connection through communication, and instead discover, or rediscover, a passion for product. This means not just having product performance as one thing on a long to-do list, but making it a top priority. And it means refusing to give up on product performance as a source of advantage over retailer own-label.

Interestingly, many of the examples I have come across where product passion is alive and kicking come from companies often championed as examples of emotional branding.

Take Innocent, for example, a brand that has managed to keep a leading 68% share of the smoothie market despite a host of own-label imitations. Most analyses of the brand's success in growing to a £l00 million plus business focus on the brand's distinctive personality and tone of voice. Of course the emotional side of the brand does shine through the brand's marketing mix. There is the now famous pack copy that reads like a mini-magazine full of jokes and stories, and the caps that, instead of having 'use by' dates printed on them, invite us to 'Enjoy by'. Then there are the distinctive promotions, such as the bottles wearing knitted hats to raise money for Help the Aged, and the recent 'Buy one, get one tree' packs.

Innocent has been lauded for its marketing techniques, but at the heart of its success is a great product.

However, when I visited Fruit Towers to meet Innocent's creative genius, Dan Germain, what struck me was how central the product was in the company. A great product is the foundation of the brand's success, and at the heart of all it does. When I signed the visitor book, I was asked to write my name and company. But I was also asked my favourite smoothie flavour. The receptionist then invited me to help myself from the fully stocked fridge of smoothies.

Looking round the open-plan office I could see that most of the people working there had done just that. This sounds simple, but many companies seem to be staffed by marketing people who don't use the brand's products unless they have to. Here are some of the ways the company invests in creating and keeping the focus firmly on product:

- Hiring top food scientists as 'fruitologists', specialising in a specific type of fruit and how to get the tastiest ones. They are experts in where to source the best fruit and the effects of seasonality on fruit taste.
- Monthly blind-testing of products against those of the competition are used to ensure Innocent stays ahead of the game, and especially of own-label products.
- Upgrading the existing flavours to make them even better, such as adding 'six extra strawberries' in the strawberry and banana one.
- Having a kitchen right in the middle of the office, where new recipes are created, and where anyone in the company can roll up their sleeves and have a go.
- Looking for new and interesting fruits, such as those in the new Superfruit range that have extra functional, health-related benefits.

2 Leave the ladder in the garage

The biggest problem with the laddering approach is the risk of us creating emotionally-based communication with no link back to the product. This creates 'sponsored entertainment', where people remember the execution more than they do the brand. A more effective approach is where the functional and emotional sides of the brand work together and reinforce one another. This involves finding a product truth and then telling a story about this in an emotionally involving and impactful way.

Food porn? Ads for an M&S chocolate desert increased sales by 288%.

Marks & Spencer

One of the best examples of communication combining sausage and sizzle is the hugely successful relaunch of Marks & Spencer, a story sold by marketing director Steven Sharp at a Marketing Society event earlier this year. The 'Your M&S' campaign was part of the relaunch that helped drive full-year profits to April 2006 up from £505.5m to £745.7m.

Sharp told how the first stage of the campaign featured food products, where M&S had always been strong, and in particular that chocolate pudding. The 'food porn' advertising lingered over oozing chocolate and dripping butter, using a memorable piece of music and voice-over to boost recognition and appetite appeal, increasing sales by 288%. Communication on the clothing range with Twiggy and friends only started in force a year later, after redesign work on the range had been completed. Again, this had emotional appeal, but it was built of a great product range.

Lush

The potency of combining sausage and sizzle is also shown by brands that have grown with little or no advertising. The Innocent brand discussed earlier is one of these, with sales now over the £100 million mark. Another example is the Lush brand of 'Fresh, Handmade Cosmetics'. Its products are unique on several dimensions, being made by hand, highly indulgent, not tested on animals and free of chemical preservatives.

The brand's personality and tone of voice flows from these product truths, which work to reinforce them. Each product has a picture of the person who made it on the pack or, where there is no pack, on a sign in the store, strengthening the communication of the handmade nature of the brand. As with Innocent, much attention is paid to the copy used to name and describe products. For example, the Haagenbath is described as 'a refreshing minty, pink, slow-fizzing, creamy bath bomb with grated chocolate bath melt for extra skin softening'. And the brand's product story and personality is also dramatised in activation activities, such as the 'Packaging is rubbish' campaign. Lush store staff promoted the fact that 75% of all Lush products are 'naked', with no packaging, by going to work dressed in nothing but a branded apron!

Lush stores perfectly reflect the brand personality

3 Stretch selectively

The right discipline is to launch products that not only fit with the brand idea, but also actively dramatise and reinforce it to deliver added value. One way of helping ensure the brand stretches selectively and correctly is to define the 'product DNA' (as well as the brand DNA) – the features and attributes that every new product should have.

For many years Dove had plans for a deodorant. However, it launched the product only when it was able to combine top odour protection with the brand's trademark skin mildness and one-quarter moisturising cream. Many of Lush's customers asked the brand to make a toothpaste, and the company saw a clear business opportunity. However, the launch did not happen, as the team could not find the right supplier who had a product with ingredients that had not been tested on animals.

The other important question is, of course, how effective the new extension will be at driving growth. It is tempting to launch extensions that are believed to be 'great for the brand image', despite being small in sales. This rarely works in reality. Producing 'dwarf' products steals attention and resources from the core business. Better to focus on fewer, bigger extensions that grow the brand by growing the business, such as Pampers' Active Fit nappies. These provided improved wetness protection for babies who are starting to crawl. The launch helped the brand grow its share of the UK market by 10%, at the same time as dramatising the brand idea of 'Being with you every step of the way as your baby develops and grows'.

4 Grow the core

Stretching more selectively is one way of delivering more substance. However, even better is growing the core business.

The first challenge in growing the core business is sticking to what made you famous in the first place, while updating the brand to make it fresh and relevant for today. James Bond is a good example of a brand that has done this. The latest movie, *Casino Royale*, smashed all box office records for the Bond franchise, with the opening UK weekend take of £13 million up 40% on the previous high. A look back over the history of the Bond brand shows how a number of key equities have been maintained and refreshed.

- The 'brand proposition' of 'Bond beats the baddie' is still there, though Bond is not directly 'saving the world' as in some other films. This time it's a battle of wits with a terrorist banker.
- Girls: still lots of beautiful women, but Vesper Lynd continues the trend of being a smarter, stronger Bond woman, not just a pretty face.
- The catchphrases: some of these are still here, but used in a creative way. After a near-death experience, a barman asks Bond if he wants his Martini shaken, not stirred. Daniel Craig replies, 'Do I look like I give a shit?'

- Hard man: this Bond is a rough and tough killing machine. The violence is a lot more real, and we even see Bond being bruised and beaten.

The other trick in growing the core is to redirect the creativity used in launching new products onto finding ways to activate new users and/or usage occasions. This approach helped the Axe/Lynx brand boost its business by 20% in Latin America. The team there saw that consumption per capita in one market (Argentina) was much higher than another (Brazil). When they dug into the data, the reason seemed to be young guys spraying their whole body, not just under their arms. This led to a campaign called 'Spray More, Get More', which encouraged all-over usage with the promise of, er, more sex.

What gets in the way?

The steps proposed above may seem obvious and merely the application of common sense. However, a quick look at the marketing going on today is enough to show that they are not being applied consistently. So, what gets in the way?

As mentioned earlier, emotional branding is definitely the flavour of the month, and much more fashionable than going back to basics and getting the product right.

But a bigger issue is the old problem of how little time marketers spend in a job. Firing the ad agency and making a splashy new ad that raises your profile is a more attractive option than the hard work of fixing the product when you know you will be onto your next job in a year or two.

And things get even worse when you move into the world of service branding, such as financial services. Here the changes to service culture and infrastructure take many millions of pounds and years to take effect, requiring more stamina than most of us possess. This is especially true when in reality many 'marketing' jobs in big service companies are actually communication roles, with ownership of the actual service proposition sitting in other functional silos.

Stuart Rose is a British businessman whose retail career began to take off when he joined Marks & Spencer in 1972 as a management trainee. He influenced retailing through his work with Arcadia, Debenhams and Argos and became Chief Executive of M&S in 2004.

Terry Leahy started his Tesco life working in his school holidays. He always had a keen eye for retail activity and finally became the CEO of Tesco in 1997.

Substance not spin

Ultimately, as with most of marketing and business in general, delivering more substance and less spin comes down to leadership. If you lead a product brand in a consumer goods company, you can make a huge difference to the way the brand is run, constantly challenging your team to ask, 'Where's the sausage?'

The individuals behind two of the highest-profile global marketing stories of recent years, Dove and Persil/Omo ('Dirt is Good') were both proactive in asking to stay much longer than the normal couple of years on their respective brands. Another common theme is the passion and conviction they had for their brands, and the way they drove this through the whole marketing mix, including product innovation and packaging, not just communication.

The challenge in service businesses is harder, but not impossible, as shown by the leading role played by Steven Sharp at M&S and Tim

Mason at Tesco. In addition, a CEO who believes in substance not spin is crucial, as is the case with Stuart Rose and Terry Leahy respectively.

But whatever level in the businesses we work at, we all have a role to play. And the next time we find ourselves 'doing a Hugo', we can choose instead to ask 'Where's the sausage?

David Taylor is founder and managing partner of The Brandgym, and author of four branding books including Where's the Sausage? Branding based on substance not spin.

(Source: Taylor, 2007, pp. 2–4)

Activity 4.1 Retailer brands versus product brands: who is winning?

Spend about 30 minutes on this activity.

Purpose: to consider the factors driving the development of retailer brands.

Task: What is David Taylor suggesting product brand managers can learn from retailer own brands?

Feedback

Retailers have steadily been gaining market share with own-label brands and Taylor suggests they could push manufacturer brands into second place if this trend continues. Own-label brands were considered as inferior quality to well-known brand names but recently this has changed and consumer perceptions are that the retailers (with whom they may have a long established trading relationship) now provide superior quality products at lower prices than manufacturer brands. Taylor also suggests that retailers have focused on getting the products *right* rather than relying on the consumer buying into emotive communications messages. Notwithstanding this comment, retailers have also used very creative communication advertising campaigns (e.g., M&S 'food porn') but only when they have ensured that the product on offer is what the customer needs and wants.

4.3 Types of retail brands

As you will appreciate after reading the article by Taylor, retail brands now play a more strategic role than they have done in the past. However, you also need to realise that there are many different types of retailer brands and it is important to differentiate between them in order to understand the role of particular types in retail strategies (Varley and Rafiq, 2004). Table 4.2 shows a typology of retail own brands.

Table 4.2 A typology of retail own brands

Own-brand type	Description	Identification with the retailer	Positioning	Product range
Generics	Non-branded merchandise sold in plain packaging with low-price positioning; now replaced by budget own brands (see below)	Limited	Low	Limited
Controlled brands or exclusive manufacturer brands	Brands owned by a manufacturer but exclusive to a retailer in a given market, e.g. Procter & Gamble's Physique haircare brand sold exclusively through Tesco	None	Low/ medium	Limited
Counter brands	Brands owned by a retailer, differentiated by product category; the retailer is not identified and little attempt is made to associate the brand with them, e.g. Matsui brand sold in Currys and Dixons	None	Low/ medium	Limited
Budget brands	Products identified with the retailer but which stress the name of the good itself; sold in relatively simple packaging with low-price positioning, e.g. Tesco Value brands	Strong	Medium	Limited
Copycat brands: Reengineered brands	Low-cost retailer-owned brands offering the same functionality as the branded product, e.g. Tesco Healthy Living tomato soup mimics the Weight Watchers soups introduced by Heinz	Strong	Low/ medium	Wide
Lookalikes	Offering similar quality to manufacturer brands and imitating many of their visual features, e.g. Sainsbury's Classic Cola	Medium	Medium	Limited
House brands	The name of the retailer appears together with a separate brand name for different product groups, e.g. Tesco Finest range	Strong	Medium	Wide
Exclusive designer labels	Products designed exclusively for the retailer and carrying the designer's name, e.g. Jasper Conran at Debenhams	Strong	High	Limited
Fascia brands	The trade name of the retailer (or a name strongly associated with them, e.g. St Michael and Marks & Spencer) identifies all products sold as private brands, e.g. Next	Very strong	Medium/ high	Wide

(Source: adapted from Varley and Rafiq, 2004, p. 209, based on Pellegrini, 1993)

According to Varley and Rafiq (2004, p. 208), this typology suggests an own-brand development strategy: retailers can start with generics and then move up the own-brand ladder as they gain experience and confidence in own-brand development. William and Jary (1997) suggested a similar staged development of own brands in which, over time, retailers trade up in terms of quality and relative price compared with manufacturer brands. They begin with generics followed by cheap store brands, which are a step above generics although still of lower quality and much cheaper than manufacturer brands.

Lidl's GranArom own-brand coffee

Reengineered low-cost brands are the next step up. In this case, the retailer proactively examines the branded product and packaging to see how costs can be reduced, whilst offering the same functionality. The retailer makes no real attempt to pass off the product as a copycat of the branded product. For example, discount retailer Aldi has developed a set of exclusive brands which it sells at prices 20 to 30 per cent lower than other supermarkets across the range.

The next stage is to offer 'par quality' store brands, which are aimed to match manufacturer brands in terms of quality and performance but at prices 10 to 25 per cent lower. The price discount is possible because retailers' marketing expenses are considerably lower and they can subcontract production of the store brands to manufacturers with excess capacity.

In the final stages, retail brands take on a leadership role through positioning and innovation with price parity or a premium price relative to manufacturer brands and hence better margins than traditional own labels (Dunne and Narasimhan, 1999).

4.4 Retail brands and own-label brands

The typology of brands proposes strategic options for a retailer but it is important to consider how own brands impact on the retail brand itself so that the retailer can maintain a balance between the total retail brand, own brands and manufacturer brands. Failure to do this can affect market share. Major grocery retailers such as Sainsbury's have lost market share in the past due to having too high a proportion of own-brand products in their ranges.

The next activity involves reading an article about how to understand retail branding by Ailawadi and Keller, which was published in the *Journal of Retailing*, a leading marketing academic journal. The article, 'Understanding retail branding: conceptual insights and research priorities', is a literature review, which means that the authors have looked at a whole range of articles discussing branding from a retail perspective and have analysed and distilled these readings to produce a focused article discussing retail branding.

Activity 4.2 Understanding retail branding Part 1

Spend about 20 minutes on this activity.

Purpose: the purpose of the following three activities is to extend your understanding of retail branding, to learn about the difference between products as brands and retailers as brands, and to develop your reading and analytical skills.

Task: Set out below is the text from an academic article published in the *Journal of Retailing* by Ailawadi and Keller. Read the introductory section and, as you read, imagine you are a retailer thinking about how to develop your company's brand. Then answer the question that follows the reading. The article has been split into sections to help you develop your skills in reading this type of material.

Essential Reading 1 – Understanding retail branding: conceptual insights and research priorities.

Retailers as brands

The last decade has seen major flux in retailing, especially in the US grocery and general merchandise industry. On one hand, the growth of promotions and private labels has been seen by many as an indicator of growing retailer power. On the other hand, the growth of discounters and warehouse clubs has put immense pressure on traditional retailers and significantly increased retail competition both within and between retail formats. Since a large portion of most retailers' revenue and profit comes from selling manufacturer brands, which many of their competitors also offer, building their own equity is a particularly challenging problem, but one with big potential rewards. Such equity insulates them from competing retailers, which has the direct impact of increasing revenue and profitability, and the indirect impact of decreasing costs as their leverage with brand manufacturers also increases.

Although many important branding principles apply, retailer brands are sufficiently different from product brands that the actual application of those branding principles can vary. Retailer brands are typically more multi-sensory in nature than product brands and can rely on rich consumer experiences to impact their equity. Retailers also create their brand images in different ways, e.g., by attaching unique associations to the quality of their service, their product assortment and merchandising, pricing and credit policy, etc.

In most consumer industries, the image and equity of retailer brands also depends on the manufacturer brands they carry and the equity of those brands. Retailers use manufacturer brands to generate consumer interest, patronage, and loyalty in a store. Manufacturer brands operate almost as 'ingredient brands' that wield significant consumer pull, often more than the retailer brand does. To the extent 'you are what you sell', manufacturer brands help to create an image and establish a positioning for the store.

At the same time, retailers compete with manufacturers for consumer pull to increase their relative market power and their share of the total channel profit pie (Steiner 1993). In doing so, they may sell some of their own brands. In fact, in industries like apparel, one can find several examples of retailers who carry only their own private label products, e.g., GAP, Brooks Brothers, and Talbots. Private label products may have their own unique brand names or be branded under the name of the retailer. They allow the retailer to differentiate its offerings from competing retailers, although often without the support afforded manufacturer brands.

Understanding how a retailer should be positioned and how the brand assortment sold by the retailer is related to its image are thus of critical importance. Some retailers have managed their brands more effectively than others, as is evident in their performance. For instance, although overall US retail profitability did not improve during the eighties and nineties, some retailers have fared exceedingly well (Ailawadi, Borin, & Farris 1995).

The purpose of this article is to (1) integrate the lessons from branding and retail image research to provide a better understanding of how retailers create their brand images; (2) review what we know about how the types of brands that retailers sell – manufacturer brands and private labels – influence and are influenced by the retailers' brand image; and (3) highlight some important areas that deserve further research in the form of three sets of research priorities.

(Ailawadi and Keller, 2004, p. 332)

What has the introduction to this article told us about manufacturer (product) brands and a retailer as a brand?

Feedback

Retailers sell manufacturer brands but increasingly they are introducing private label (own brands); this is enhancing the retailers' power in the supply chain.

Retailers get good levels of profit from selling manufacturer brands but so do their competitors. Therefore, if a retailer can develop brand equity in its own right this can increase revenues and profitability.

Retailers as brands are different from products as brands because of the extent of the experiences that a customer has when visiting retail stores or encountering a retail offer.

Retailers use manufacturer brands when developing their own image and brand equity. In other words, the products a retailer sells help to define the retailer brand.

These are important issues, which highlight why it is important to understand the implications of branding in the retail industry.

Activity 4.3 Understanding retail branding Part 2

Spend about 45 minutes on this activity.

Purpose: as with the last activity, the purpose of this activity is to extend your understanding of retail branding, to learn about the difference between products as brands and retailers as brands, and to develop your reading and analytical skills.

Task: Read the following continuation of the Ailawadi and Keller article as directed and answer the question that follows the reading.

The dimensions of retailer image

Following the American Marketing Association's definition of a brand, a retail brand identifies the goods and services of a retailer and differentiates them from those of competitors. A retailer's brand equity is exhibited in consumers responding more favourably to its marketing actions than they do to those of competing retailers (Keller, 2003). The image of the retailer in the minds of consumers is the basis of this brand equity.

Researchers have studied a multitude of retailer attributes that influence overall image, e.g., the variety and quality of products, services, and brands sold; the physical store appearance, the appearance, behaviour and service quality of employees; the price levels, depth and frequency of promotions and so on. Lindquist (1974) and Mazursky and Jacoby (1986) categorised these attributes into a smaller set of location, merchandise, service, and store atmosphere related dimensions. To organise our review of the key lessons from retailer image research, we adopt this categorisation, but modify it slightly to better reflect the increasing emphasis that pricing and the breadth and depth of merchandise assortment have received in more recent research. The five dimensions we use to review past research are: (1) access, (2) in-store atmosphere, (3) price and promotion, (4) cross-category product/ service assortment, and (5) within-category brand/item assortment.

Access

The location of a store and the distance that the consumer must travel to shop there are basic criteria in their store choice decisions. Beginning with gravity models (e.g., Huff, 1966) store choice and the optimization of retail site location attracted a lot of research attention in the eighties (e.g., Achabal, Gorr, & Mahajan 1982; Donthu & Rust 1989; Ghosh & Craig 1983). Today, suburban sprawl, greater driving distances, the appearance of new warehouse retail formats that are often located in large spaces away from residential areas, and online retailing have made location somewhat less central as a store choice criterion.

Consistent with this trend, Bell, Ho, and Tang (1998) find that location no longer explains most of the variance in store choice decisions. Rather, store choice decisions seem to be consistent with a model where consumers optimize their total shopping costs, effort to access the store location being one component of their fixed cost of shopping. That is not to say, however, that location is unimportant. Consumers' store choice may be based on different criteria depending upon the nature of the trip, for instance, small basket fill-in trips are very unlikely to be made to distant or inconvenient locations. And, retailers in some formats, like convenience, drug, or supermarket have less flexibility in their location decision than mass merchandisers or warehouse clubs.

In summary, although location no longer explains a major portion of the variance in consumers' choice of stores, it is a key component in consumers' assessment of total shopping costs and is still important for retailers who wish to get a substantial share of wallet from fill-in trips and small basket shoppers.

Store atmosphere

Mehrabian and Russell (1974) note that the response that atmosphere elicits from consumers varies along three main dimensions of pleasantness, arousal, and dominance. This response, in turn, influences behaviour, with greater likelihood of purchase in more pleasant settings and in settings of intermediate arousal level. Different elements of a retailer's in-store environment, e.g., colour, music, and crowding, can influence consumers' perceptions of a store's atmosphere, whether or not they visit a store, how much time they spend in it, and how much money they spend there (Bellizzi, Crowley, & Hasty 1983; Eroglu & Machleit 1990; Grewal, Barker, Levy, & Voss 2003; Milliman 1982). Baker, Parsuraman, Grewal, and Voss (2002) provide a good review of this research and categorize the elements of in-store atmosphere into physical features like design, lighting, and layout, ambient features like music and smell, and social features like type of clientele, employee availability and friendliness. They note that atmosphere can affect consumers' perceptions of the economic and psychological costs of shopping in a store and find that pleasing physical design lowers both economic and psychological costs while music lowers the latter.

Store atmosphere mediates consumer perceptions of other dimensions of store image. For instance, Baker et al. (2002) find that store environment factors, particularly physical design perceptions, significantly affect consumers' perceptions of merchandise price, merchandise quality, and employee service quality. Schlosser (1998) argues that, since store atmosphere has a social identity appeal, a pleasing atmosphere in the store should influence perceptions of socially communicative products in the store, not so much intrinsically rewarding products. This logic can be extended to argue that store atmosphere would have a greater impact on perceptions of products with higher perceived (social) risk. Indeed, Richardson, Jain, and Dick (1996) do find that consumers' ratings of the private label's quality are higher when the store is aesthetically pleasing than when it is less attractive, although there is no significant difference in their ratings of national brands' quality.

In summary, a pleasing in-store atmosphere provides substantial hedonic utility to consumers and encourages them to visit more often, stay longer, and buy more. Although it also improves consumers' perceptions of the quality of merchandise in the store, consumers tend to associate it with higher prices. From a branding perspective, an appealing in-store atmosphere offers much potential in terms of crafting a unique store image and establishing differentiation. Increasingly, brands are being positioned on the basis of their intangibles and attributes and benefits that transcend product or service performance. Even if the products and brands stocked by a retailer are similar to others, the ability to create a strong in-store personality and rich experiences can play a crucial role in building retailer brand equity.

Price and promotion

No matter how the characteristics of the consumer, product, store, or purchase situation might differ, price represents the monetary expenditure that the consumer must incur in order to make a purchase. From the vast literature on pricing, we highlight three areas that are of direct relevance to consumers' image and choice of retailers.

Store price perceptions

A retailer's price image should be influenced by attributes like average level of prices, how much variation there is in prices over time, the frequency and depth of promotions, and whether the retailer positions itself as EDLP [every day low price] or HILO [high–low promotional pricing]. Decades ago, however, Brown (1969) highlighted the difference between consumers' perceptions of price levels in various stores and reality, showing that consumers may use non-price related cues like service offerings and quality levels to form their price perceptions. That consumers may not form valid perceptions of actual prices in a store is supported by Dickson and Sawyer's (1990) widely cited work, but consumers do develop some general price perceptions of products in a store, and can evaluate their expensiveness in relative terms (Monroe & Lee 1999).

Desai and Talukdar (2003) develop a product-price saliency framework to examine how consumers form an overall store price image (OSPI). They show that products with high unit prices and high purchase frequency are more salient and therefore contribute more to OSPI, with purchase frequency dominating unit price in importance. Alba, Broniarczyk, Shimp, and Urbany (1994) examine how consumers' perceptions of store prices change with prior beliefs and information about how frequently a store has a price advantage on a set of products and the magnitude of that price advantage. They find that, although prior beliefs affect price perceptions, frequency of price advantage dominates both prior beliefs and magnitude of price advantage in influencing consumers' perceptions of store price level.

Retailer pricing format

A retailer's price format, which is on a continuum between Every Day Low Price (EDLP) and High-Low Promotional Pricing (HILO), also influences consumers' store choice and shopping behaviour. Bell and Lattin (1998) show that 'large basket shoppers' prefer EDLP stores whereas 'small basket shoppers' prefer HILO stores. The intuition behind the finding is straightforward. Large basket shoppers are captive to the pricing across a large set of product categories at a time and do not have the flexibility to take advantage of occasional price deals on individual products. They therefore prefer EDLP because it gives them a lower expected price for their shopping basket. Small basket shoppers, on the other hand, can take advantage of variations in prices of individual products and, by buying on deal, can lower their basket price even if average prices in the store are high.

Ho, Tang, and Bell (1998) also explain why both EDLP and HILO co-exist in the market. They show that average prices are higher in HILO stores and average purchase quantities are lower. HILO pricing is more effective in enticing shoppers to make more frequent store visits, but, since shoppers have the flexibility to buy more on trips when prices are lower, the HILO store's revenue per unit time is lower. In contrast, EDLP decreases shopping frequency but generates higher revenue per unit time. Thus, neither format is dominant.

Price promotion induced store switching

The third research area studies whether retailer price promotions result in store switching by consumers. Kumar and Leone (1988) and Walters (1991) find a significant impact of promotions on store switching/traffic. However, it is unlikely that consumers would keep track of weekly promotions on a multitude of categories in all the stores in their neighbourhood. Bucklin and Lattin (1992) show that retail promotions in any one category do not directly influence a consumer's store choice decision, but they indirectly affect where the category is purchased. Consumers typically shop in more than one store. They may purchase a promoted product in the store they happen to be visiting whereas they would otherwise have purchased it in another store. This also reiterates the important moderating effect of in-store atmosphere. The impact of promotions will be higher in a pleasant atmosphere because the longer consumers stay in a store, the more likely they are to notice promotions and buy more than planned during the shopping trip.

In summary, consumers are more likely to develop a favourable price image when retailers offer frequent discounts on a large number of products than when they offer less frequent, but steeper discounts. Further, products that have high unit price and are purchased more frequently are more salient in determining the retailer's price image. One pricing format does not dominate another, but large basket shoppers prefer EDLP stores while small basket shoppers prefer HILO, and it is optimal for HILO stores to charge an average price that is higher than the EDLP. Finally, price promotions are associated with store switching but the effect is indirect, altering consumers' category purchase decisions while they are in the store rather than altering their choice of which store to visit.

These findings are crucial for retailers who are trying to build their retail brand. They highlight the levers that retailers can use to influence their price image and the impact of their price promotions, and they show that retailers have considerable flexibility in following different pricing strategies and avoiding head-to-head price competitions with other retailers even though they may carry many of the very same manufacturer brands that competing retailers carry.

Cross-category assortment

Consumers' perceptions of the breadth of different products and services offered by a retailer under one roof significantly influence store image. The benefits of a wide assortment are clear. First, the greater the breadth of product assortment, the greater the range of different situations in which the retailer is recalled and considered by the consumer, and therefore the stronger its salience. As noted by Keller (2003), salience is the most basic building block for a brand. Second, the one-stop shopping convenience that a broad product assortment enables is becoming more important than ever for today's time-constrained consumer (Messinger & Narasimhan 1997), putting pressure on retailers to broaden their assortment. Third, consumers regularly shop at more than one store, and, as noted earlier, they may purchase a category in the store that they are visiting based on in-store assortment and marketing mix activities whereas they would otherwise have purchased it in another store. Together with the fact that unplanned purchases comprise a significant portion of consumers' total shopping basket, this gives an advantage to retailers with broader assortments.

The branding literature, however, suggests some potential pitfalls of broad assortments, apart from the rather obvious downside that increasing assortment breadth brings with it significantly higher costs for the retailer. Inman, Shankar, and Ferraro (2004) show that certain types of product categories have 'signature' associations with specific channels, e.g., supermarkets with food, drug channels with medications and health products, and mass merchandisers with household items. But, research has shown that a brand that is seen as prototypical of a product category can be difficult to extend outside the category

(Farquhar & Herr 1993). Therefore, if a retailer has strong signature associations with certain categories, consumers may find it difficult to think of the retailer in connection with other, very different categories. Brand extensions research also shows that a large number of associations could produce interference effects and lower memory performance (Meyers-Levy 1989).

The good news, however, is that if the retailer attempts to sell a new line of products or offer a new service that fails to connect with consumers, there may be little long-term harm as long as the new line is not too closely connected to the retailer's signature categories or its own brand name. Research on brand equity dilution has found that parent brands generally are not particularly vulnerable to failed brand extensions: An unsuccessful brand extension potentially damages a parent brand only when there is a high degree of similarity or 'fit' involved (Ahluwalia & Gürhan-Canli 2000; Gürhan-Canli & Maheswaran 1998; Keller & Aaker 1992). Of course, the retailer's image and reputation would be more vulnerable if the expanded product assortment is a private label branded under the store's own name.

Another finding from brand extension research is also relevant to retailers' assortment decisions. Keller and Aaker (1992) showed that by taking 'little steps', i.e., by introducing a series of closely related but increasingly distant extensions, it is possible for a brand to ultimately enter product categories that would have been much more difficult, or perhaps even impossible, to have entered directly (Dawar & Anderson 1994; Jap 1993; Meyvis & Janiszewski, 2004). Successfully introduced brand extensions can lead to enhanced perceptions of corporate credibility and improved evaluations of even more dissimilar brand extensions that are introduced later. In other words, retailers are most likely to be successful if they expand their meaning and assortment in gradual stages, as for example Amazon, or even Walmart, did.

In summary, a broad assortment can create customer value by offering convenience and ease of shopping. It is risky to extend too far too soon, but, staying too tightly coupled to the current assortment and image may unnecessarily limit the retailer's range of experimentation (Danneels 2003). The logic and sequencing of a retailer's assortment policy are critical to its ability to successfully expand its meaning and appeal to consumers over time.

Within-category assortment

Consumers' perceptions of the depth of a retailer's assortment within a product category are an important dimension of store image and a key driver of store choice. As the perceived assortment of brands, flavours, and sizes increases, variety seeking consumers will perceive greater utility (Kahn & Wansink 2004; McAlister & Pessemier 1982), consumers with uncertain future preferences will believe they have more flexibility in their choices (Kahn & Lehmann 1991), and, in general, it is more likely that consumers will find the item they desire. More offerings in a category, however, can be costly both for the retailer and the consumer. From the viewpoint of the retailer, cutting out 20 percent of the most inefficient items from its assortment can mean savings of several million dollars per year for a large chain. From the viewpoint of the consumer, researchers like Greenleaf and Lehmann (1995), Tversky and Shafir (1992) and Iyengar and Lepper (2000) argue that increasing the choice set leads to cognitive overload and uncertainty and can actually decrease the likelihood of purchase. In recent years, therefore, researchers have focused on how consumers perceive an assortment and whether and how actual assortment can be reduced without adversely affecting consumer perceptions.

Kahn and Lehmann (1991), Hoch, Bradlow, and Wansink (1999), and Boatwright and Nunes (2001) highlight, for example, the importance of uniqueness or differences in attribute levels among items, with greater uniqueness being associated with greater perceived variety in assortment. Kahn and Wansink (2004) show that the organization and symmetry of an assortment moderate the impact of actual assortment variety on perceived variety and consumption, with organized and asymmetric assortments having a more positive effect.

Broniarczyk, Hoyer, and McAlister (1998) find that SKU [stock-keeping unit] reduction does not lower consumers' perceptions of assortment much unless their favourite item is dropped or the total amount of space devoted to the category is reduced. Further, a moderate decrease in number of SKUs can actually increase consumers' perceptions of assortment as long as their favourite item and total category space are maintained. Dreze, Hoch, and Purk (1994) and Boatwright and Nunes (2001), do find that aggregate sales actually increase when less popular SKUs are deleted.

In summary, greater perceived assortment does influence store image, store choice, and satisfaction with the store, but a greater number of SKUs need not directly translate to better perceptions. Retailers can reduce the number of SKUs substantially without adversely affecting consumer perceptions, as long as they pay attention to the most preferred brands, the organization of the assortment and the availability of diverse product attributes.

Brand assortment

One specific aspect of the retailer's assortment strategy, brand assortment, has become particularly important in the last decade as a tool for retailers to influence their image and develop their own brand name. Most retailers carry manufacturer brands, but, increasingly, they also offer private label products. One motivation for offering private labels is the higher percent margins that they provide to retailers (Hoch & Banerji 1993); another is the negotiating leverage they provide over manufacturers (Narasimhan & Wilcox 1998); and a third is the implicit assumption that providing a private label brand engenders loyalty to the retailer (Steenkamp & Dekimpe 1997).

The growth in private labels has spawned much research on who buys private label products, whether and how private labels provide leverage to retailers, and the category and market determinants of private label share. We review the main findings from this research and summarize the implications for retail branding. We also review the rather small body of research that throws light on whether and how the manufacturer brands carried by a retailer influence consumers' evaluation of private label products.

(Ailawadi and Keller, 2004, pp.332–6)

Activity 4.3 continued

What are the key lessons a retailer needs to understand when developing a retail brand?

Feedback

From a branding perspective, location is not important as a single discriminating factor of where individuals shop, but in certain buying situations, for example convenience and top-up shopping, location can have an influence.

Store atmosphere encourages shoppers to visit a store, so it is important when developing a retail brand to create the right atmosphere in the store.

Pricing strategies and promotional discounts are important. It is vital to achieve a balance between pricing, discounts and promotions.

Product ranges are also key to creating a retail brand. A retailer should aim to create product ranges which are sufficiently broad and yet focused to meet consumers' needs.

Product assortment also influences store image, store choice and customer satisfaction. Retailers can reduce the assortment but must be aware of the customers' favourite brands.

Activity 4.4 Understanding retail branding Part 3

Spend about 30 minutes on this activity and then about 30 minutes reading the final section of this reading.

Purpose: as with the two previous activities, you will be using this activity to extend your understanding of retail branding, to learn about the difference between products as brands and retailers as brands, and to develop your reading and analytical skills.

Task: Read this part of the article as directed and answer the question that follows the reading.

Private labels

Although the growth of private labels has been interpreted by some as a sign of the 'decline of brands', it could easily be argued that the *opposite* conclusion is more valid, as private label growth could be seen in some ways as a consequence of cleverly designed branding strategies.

One of the most fundamental questions that researchers have asked about private labels is 'Who is the private label prone consumer?' Interestingly, despite a large body of research on this issue (e.g., Ailawadi, Gedenk, & Nelsin 2001; Richardson et al. 1996), we have few empirical generalizations about the characteristics of the private label user. The best we can say is that s/he is price sensitive but not image sensitive, middle-income, and educated.

Another key question is 'Do private labels give retailers negotiating leverage over national brand manufacturers?' Several analytical models have been developed in recent years that claim the answer to this question is 'yes' (Mills 1995; Narasimhan & Wilcox 1998), and Ailawadi and Harlam's (2004) empirical analysis supports the hypothesis that retailers are able to earn high margins on national brands in categories where their private label has a high share.

A third question relates to the category characteristics that are conducive to private label success. Several researchers have noted that private label proneness is more category specific than consumer specific (e.g., Sethuraman 1992; Sethuraman & Cole 1997). Private labels gain a higher share in large, less-promoted categories with a small number of brands, and when the price differential between national brands and private label is large (Dhar & Hoch 1998; Hoch & Banerji 1993; Sethuraman 1992). But, the most important driver of private label share is its perceived quality (Hoch & Banerji 1993; Sethuraman 2000).

The fact that the perceived quality differential between private labels and national brands is so important clearly means that the better the private label position in terms of quality, the more likely it is to succeed. However, should the private label be positioned against the leading national brand? Sayman, Hoch, and Raju (2002) show analytically that it is profitable for the private label to position itself close to the leading national brand, particularly when the leading brand has a high share. Empirically, they find that, when private labels do target a particular national brand, they tend to target the leading brand. Interestingly, though, both Sayman et al. (2002) and Sethuraman (2002) find that the majority of private labels do not seem to target a particular national brand, perhaps because that positioning may not be credible.

Is private label use related to store loyalty? The answer has direct relevance to the ability of private labels to help build retailers' brands. Conventional wisdom certainly has it that store image and loyalty may improve as consumers become familiar with the private label and their shopping is facilitated by the ability to buy a single brand across a wide range of product categories (e.g., Steenkamp & Dekimpe 1997). Corstjens and Lal (2000) also show analytically that the ability to engender store loyalty can make private labels profitable for retailers even if they do not have a cost advantage. However, empirical evidence of the relationship between private label use and store loyalty is not only sparse but mixed.

Corstjens and Lal (2000) provide empirical evidence of a positive correlation between private label use and store loyalty using scanner data for one product category, and Ailawadi et al. (2001) show a positive association using survey data. On the other hand, Ailawadi and Harlam (2004) find that heavy private label users buy significantly less from a retailer than do medium private label users. Further, none of these studies can attest to the direction of causality in the relationship. As a result, it is by no means clear that private labels increase consumer loyalty to a retailer's stores.

In summary, private label users span a wide array of demographic and psychographic characteristics, so retailers who use a strong private label strategy are not limiting themselves to only a narrow section of the market. The negotiating leverage provided by a successful private label can make it easier for a retailer to strengthen some of the other levers of brand image, e.g., more attractive prices and promotions for the best national brands. There is significant variation in private label share across categories, and the quality differential with national brands is a much more important driver of share than the price differential. But, it is not clear whether private labels really improve store loyalty, and though analytical research suggests that positioning next to the leading brand is a smart strategy for maximizing category profit, it is not clear whether such positioning is credible in the minds of consumers.

(Ailawadi and Keller, 2004, p.336)

Activity 4.4 continued

Who buys private brands?

Feedback

The private label buyer is price-sensitive but not image-sensitive, is in the middle-income range and is educated, but these criteria apply to a wide range of demographic profiles.

Now that you have completed the activities read the following box, which concludes this article by Ailawadi and Keller.

The impact of manufacturer brands on private label success

Since consumers' representations of private labels, which are not advertised much and vary from one retailer to another, may not be as well elaborated as their representations of well known manufacturer brands, extrinsic cues are more likely to affect perceptions of private labels. The manufacturer brands carried by the retailer can serve as one important extrinsic cue.

The quality of manufacturer brands positively influences consumers' image of the retailer. In turn, strong retailer image spills over to improve ratings of private label products. Jacoby and Mazursky (1984) find that carrying strong brands can improve the image of a retailer although strong retailer image cannot improve the image of a weak brand. And, Richardson et al. (1996) find that consumers' ratings of private labels are higher when store image is favourable although their ratings of manufacturer brands are not affected by store image. Simmons, Bickart, and Buchanan's (2000) analysis of whether the presence of high equity brands increases the economic value of less established brands also suggests that stocking high quality manufacturer brands can help retailers improve the performance of their private label products.

However, the influence of manufacturer brands on private label evaluation and choice may vary depending upon the assortment of price quality tiers and display structure in the store. Simonson and Tversky (1992) show that adding an even higher quality option to an existing assortment leads consumers to prefer a higher quality, higher price option, with the cheapest option losing the most. On the other hand, adding a lower quality option does not shift choices to lower quality levels. This reiterates the importance of quality in private label success and shows that the strategy of stocking an even lower quality manufacturer brand to make a low quality private label look more appealing will not be effective.

Simonson and Tversky (1992) also show that consumers choose middle or compromise alternatives in some cases but not in others. Simonson (1999) proposes that compromises are chosen when the dimensions on which choices vary have diminishing marginal values whereas non-compromise options are chosen when marginal values are increasing. Given that most private labels in US packaged goods are not positioned at the extremes, this may explain why they perform better in utilitarian versus hedonic categories.

Nowlis and Simonson (1997) show that low price, low equity brands are more likely to be chosen when they are displayed alongside competing options while high price, high equity brands are more likely to be chosen when they are displayed separately. In seeming contradiction, Simmons et al. (2000) find that, when unfamiliar brands share the retail portfolio with well known brands, the former do better in separate displays than in mixed displays. A key difference between the studies is that, in the latter, the unfamiliar brand is described to be identical to the high equity brand, generally even in price, whereas Nowlis and Simonson's low tier brands are low equity and low price. Thus, mixed displays may help the private label when it has a lower price and superior features compared to the higher equity manufacturer brands, because comparisons are easier. Otherwise, separate displays may be better because they reduce consumers' ability to use informational cues from manufacturer brands.

In summary, stocking high quality manufacturer brands improves the valuation of a retailer's private label by improving consumer perceptions of the retailer's overall image. However, the assortment of price quality tiers that the retailer carries and displays along with the private label can influence private label choice. Positioning the private label as a compromise between high and low tier manufacturer brands may increase its share in some categories but not in others. And, whether a mixed or separate display is better for private labels may depend upon whether it has superior price and product features.

Future research priorities

The above review highlights several insights that past research has provided into some relevant retailer branding considerations. Yet, much work clearly still needs to be done. In this concluding section, we review three areas that deserve greater research attention.

Development and application of traditional branding theory

There are a number of branding principles and concepts that could be productively applied to retailer brands. Here we highlight three important ones.

Brand personality

Much of the theory and practice of branding deals with intangibles – how marketers can transcend their physical products or service specifications to create more value. One important brand intangible is brand personality – the human characteristics or traits that can be attributed to a brand. One widely accepted brand personality scale is composed of five factors (Aaker 1996):

1. sincerity (e.g., down-to-earth, honest, wholesome, and cheerful)
2. excitement (e.g., daring, spirited, imaginative, and up-to-date)
3. competence (e.g., reliable, intelligent, and successful)
4. sophistication (e.g., upper class and charming)
5. ruggedness (e.g., outdoorsy and tough).

But, how applicable are these brand personality dimensions to retail brands? Do other dimensions emerge? Which retailer attributes affect which dimensions of retailer brand personality and how does this vary across market segments?

Experiential marketing

An important trend in marketing is experiential marketing – company-sponsored activities and programs designed to create daily or special brand-related interactions. Schmitt (1999, 2003) has developed the concept of Customer Experience Management (CEM) – which he defines as the process of strategically managing a customer's entire experience with a product or company.

Retailers are obviously in an ideal position to create experiences for their customers. These experiences may involve their own private labels or manufacturer brands, or may be tied not to a specific product but the store as a whole. A host of questions is raised by such strategies. What kinds of feelings can be engendered by a retailer's event? How can that become linked to the retailer's brand? How do retailers develop their communication strategies as a whole? Can retailers use the web to provide further event support and additional experiences?

A related issue is how retailers can engage in activities, perhaps in collaboration with national manufacturers, to encourage product use and communicate or demonstrate product information to build brand awareness and enhance brand image for the individual products or services that are sold. How can in-store merchandising, signage, displays, and other activities leverage the equity of the brands that the retailer sells while still building its own equity?

Brand architecture

Brand architecture involves defining both *brand boundaries* and *brand relationships*. The role of brand architecture is two-fold:

1. to clarify all product and service offerings and improve brand awareness with consumers
2. to motivate consumer purchase by enhancing the brand image of products and services.

In general, there are three key brand architecture tasks:

1. Defining brand potential. What can the brand stand for? What should the brand promise be? How should the brand be competitively positioned?
2. Identifying opportunities to achieve brand potential. What *products or services* are necessary to achieve the brand potential? What *markets* should be tapped to achieve growth?
3. Organizing brand offerings. How should products and services be branded so that they achieve their maximum sales and equity potential?

These tasks suggest a number of research questions. In a retailing context, brand architecture issues revolve around how many and what kind of products and services are provided by the retailer (i.e., cross- and within-category assortment) and how the various products and services are branded. An obvious question is how the retailer chooses to develop private label offerings, if at all, as described in the next section. But, several other issues need to be considered, as follows.

For example, at the store level, how can a retail brand be optimally positioned with respect to competitors? How should competition best be identified and addressed? How should the brand essence or core meaning of a retail brand be defined? How flexible are the mental categories consumers form for retail brands? Within the store, other brand architecture issues also exist. Should the retailer develop brands for different sections of the store or groups of branded products or services? How can the retailer add value to already-branded products or services? Does creating sub-brands under the retailer brand name help increase awareness or enhance the image of the brands that are being sold? Retailers need to carefully design and implement a brand architecture strategy to maximize retailer brand equity and sales.

Role of private labels in building retailer brand equity

Although researchers have discussed optimal private label introduction, quality, pricing, and positioning strategies from the perspective of private label sales or category profit maximisation, there is little work, either normative or descriptive, that links these strategic decisions to building the retailer's brand equity. We discuss below some issues that are particularly important from the perspective of retail branding.

Category determinants of private label success

What are the category and market factors that determine how effective private labels will be in building the retailer brand? Should retailers in different formats emphasise private labels in different categories? Inman et al. (2004) show that consumers associate different product categories with different retail formats. Bell et al. (1998) also argue that consumers build both category-independent and category-specific store loyalty. Would it be more effective for retailers to develop private labels in categories that consumers already associate them with or in categories that are not traditionally associated with them?

Private label tiers and retailer brand positioning

There are at least four tiers of private label products, ranging from low quality, no-name generics to cheap, medium quality own labels to somewhat less expensive, comparable quality private labels, to premium quality, high value added private labels that are not priced lower than national brands (Laaksonen & Reynolds 1994). In Europe, especially in the UK, one can find many examples of the last two tiers, most notably Marks & Spencer's or Tesco's private labels. In North America, brands such as GAP, Tiffany, Brooks Brothers, and Talbots have established strong, premium private labels, but Loblaw's Presidents Choice may be the only really successful example of a premium private label in packaged goods.

However, more retailers are attempting to create a line of private labels that spans these tiers. For instance, the supermarket retailer Kroger offers a line of three private labels – the premium quality 'Private Selection', the Kroger Brand that is guaranteed to be better than or equal to national brands, and the most economical FMV brand (For Maximum Value). Clearly, this private label portfolio strategy allows the retailer to cover a range of price-quality tiers but, how effective is it in building the retail brand? Is the retailer's ability to position his or her retail brand improved or restricted by the presence of a private label, and the tier(s) in which the private label is positioned? What types of retailers are most likely to benefit from private labels in terms of their retail brand equity?

Private label branding strategy

Many retailers give their own name to their private label, whereas others use different names for their private label products. For instance, CVS puts the 'CVS' name on all its private label products while Kmart does not. Aldi, a German hard discounter who is becoming a major force in European retailing, also does not put its own name on any of the products it sells even though only private labels are sold in its stores.

Little research has examined the effectiveness of retailer's private label branding strategy. The one exception we are aware of is Dhar and Hoch (1998) who included the private label branding decision as one of the variables in their analysis of private label market share and found that putting the retailer's own name on the private label is positively associated with private label share. What are the factors that determine whether one strategy would be more or less effective than the other? On one hand, having the same name and perhaps even the same package design for products in a wide array of categories across the store, certainly strengthens awareness and recall of the retail brand, and may facilitate the consumer's decision making. On the other hand, will consumers find it credible that the retailer can provide a good value, strong product in so many different product categories? Would it be desirable for a retailer like Aldi to have its big box, discount image be transferred to the products it sells?

Consumer perceptions of a private label product branded under the store name are more likely to colour their impressions of the store as whole – and vice versa – than if a different name were used to brand the product. Yet, the different inherent qualities of a retail store and its products suggest that the flow of meaning and equity may not always be strong. In other words, consumers may be able to mentally compartmentalise product offerings as distinct from retailing activities such that, even if they deemed a particular store brand product as unacceptable, they may be less inclined to downgrade their evaluations of the retailer as a whole. If the retailer chooses not to use the store name for private label products, the feedback effects, both positive and negative, would presumably be less strong.

Extending private labels

One of the major benefits of brand equity is the option it provides for extending the brand name to other market segments within the category or to other product categories. Although some retailers with premium private labels sell those private labels through other retail outlets (e.g., Starbucks), it is not yet common for North American packaged goods retailers to do so – they do not yet seem to have that kind of equity.

In terms of building brand equity, the key point of difference to consumers for private labels has generally been 'good value,' a desirable and transferable association across many product categories. As a result, private labels can be extremely 'broad', and their name can be applied across many different products. Research has shown that because of their intangible nature, more abstract associations may be seen as more relevant across a wide set of categories (Aaker & Keller 1990; Rangaswamy, Burke, & Oliva 1993).

But all brands have boundaries. If a retailer extends its private label assortment too far beyond the categories that consumers associate with its channel type, will the benefits be so small as to outweigh the costs of that assortment breadth? Or will such an action be particularly effective in differentiating the retailer's image from competitors in its own channel? Is a strategy of multiple private label brand names more effective from the point of view of extension than having a single private label under the store name?

Manufacturer response

Manufacturers have responded to the rise of private labels in a number of different ways: decreasing costs, cutting prices, increasing R&D expenditures, increasing promotions, introducing discount 'fighter' brands, and supplying private label makers. Hoch (1996) and Dunne and Narasimhan (1999) discuss how manufacturers should think about private labels and what issues they should consider in deciding whether to supply private label products. Ailawadi et al. (2001) show that although there is a segment of value conscious consumers who buy private labels and manufacturer brands when the latter are promoted, there are also two separate and sizeable segments that buy one but not the other. Offering deeper promotions to combat private labels may therefore not be the ideal response for manufacturers. However, more empirical analysis is needed to examine the effectiveness of different types of manufacturer response. Some manufacturers have their own outlets (e.g., Niketown, Polo) which compete with their retailers. What are the brand equity and consumer loyalty implications of manufacturer-controlled stores?

Measuring retailer brand equity

The measurement of brand equity has been one of the most challenging and important issues for both academics and managers. A common conceptual definition of brand equity and a clear distinction between the consumer-based sources of brand equity and the product-market outcomes of brand equity have been very useful in efforts to develop measures of brand equity (e.g., Ailawadi, Lehmann, & Neslin 2003; Keller & Lehmann 2002), but a single measure that offers rich insights and diagnosticity and yet is easy to compute and track still evades us.

As if the measurement of brand equity were not hard enough, the measurement of retail brand equity adds its own unique challenges. Brand equity is defined as the marketing effects or outcomes that accrue to the product or service with its brand name as compared to the outcomes if that same product or service did not have the brand name (Keller 1993). Since it is difficult to determine what outcomes would accrue in the hypothetical 'no brand name' situation, researchers often use private labels as the 'no brand name' benchmark (Ailawadi et al. 2003; Park & Srinivasan 1994; Sethuraman 2000). What should be the benchmark for assessing a retailer's equity and comparing it with other retailers?

One possibility is the approach developed by Dubin (1998, chapter 4) who uses oligopoly economic theory and a series of simplifying assumptions to derive an analytic expression for the incremental profit that a product would get with a brand name versus without a brand name. However, although Dubin does not treat the private label directly as a benchmark, it does play a role in his analysis – his expression for brand equity is a function of, among other things, the price elasticities of branded and private label products.

Another possibility might be to use a cross-retailer hedonic regression type of approach. For instance, one could regress retailer revenue or profit on various physical attributes such as location, square footage, store timings, product/service assortment, availability of private label, etc. A retailer's residual from this regression, i.e., the portion of its revenue or profit that cannot be explained by physical attributes, can be conceptualised as a measure of its retail brand equity.

A second complication in the measurement of retailer brand equity is that brand equity is supposed to enable the brand to charge a price premium. In fact, many researchers view this price premium as a measure of brand equity (Aaker 1991, 1996; Sethuraman 2000; Sethuraman & Cole 1997). However, several of the strongest retailers today, e.g., Walmart, Target, Aldi, are built squarely on a low price positioning. Clearly, the fact that these retailers charge lower prices than their competitors does not mean they do not have equity. Perhaps one way to conceptualize retail brand equity is to think in terms of the 'resources premium' that consumers are willing to expend in order to shop with the retailer. Resources may reflect financial considerations but also other factors such as distance travelled, brand or size preferences compromised, or services foregone.

Conclusion

Our contention is that branding and brand management principles can and should be applied to retail brands. Even though there has not been much academic research on retail branding *per se*, a lot of work has been done on retailer actions and consumer perceptions of retailer image that has direct relevance to branding. We reviewed academic research on five main dimensions of store image – access, in-store atmosphere, price and promotion, cross-category assortment, and within-category assortment – and integrated the major findings with lessons from branding research.

Consumer perceptions of these dimensions of retailer image can help develop strong and unique retail brand associations in the minds of consumers. They also influence the utilitarian and hedonic benefits that consumers feel they gain from retailer patronage and ultimately the price premium consumers will pay, the extra effort they will be willing to expend in order to shop the retailer, and the share of trips, share of requirement, and loyalty that the retailer enjoys. By influencing consumer preferences and shopping behaviour in these ways, retailers' image becomes an important base for their retail brand equity. The relative importance of different image dimensions and of utilitarian versus hedonic utility vary for different retail formats, different consumer segments, and even for different purchase occasions for the same consumer, thus providing ample opportunity for retail brands to differentiate themselves from one another.

Perhaps because of the lack of explicit focus, however, a number of important retail branding questions and issues are yet to be resolved. We have offered suggestions in three main areas – applications of traditional branding principles, the role of private labels in building retailer brand equity, and the measurement of retailer brand equity. We hope our discussion will stimulate progress in these and other areas of retail branding.

(Ailawadi and Keller, 2004, pp.337–40. Please note that all references for this article are included in Appendix 1.)

TGF Activity

Join your TGF and post a message about your favourite brand. Explain what you like about the brand and what it means to you.

4.5 Conclusions

This session has explored retail brands and discussed the role and importance of own-label brands showing how retailers can use brands for strategic development. The article you read in Activities 4.2–4 discussed the wider impact of retail branding and provided better understanding of how retailers create brand images.

Learning outcomes

When you have completed all the study elements for this session you should be able to:

- describe the meaning of the term 'brand'
- explain the key aspects of a brand
- discuss the difference between manufacturer and retailer brands
- identify key management considerations when developing a retail brand.

In addition you should have further developed your reading skills.

Block 3 Conclusions

In this block, you have read about retail marketing planning and the retail marketing mix, consumer behaviour, and branding in retailing. Studying Block 3 and completing the associated activities should have enabled you to develop a solid understanding of the importance of marketing in the retail industry. You have studied a range of materials, which presented theories, ideas and examples to help develop your understanding of each topic area. Each topic area is fundamental to the application of retail marketing and gives an insight into how retailing and marketing are interrelated.

In the online activities for Block 3 you have learnt about the promotional mix and how retailers use advertising, sales promotions, public relations and other techniques to communicate with their customers.

In Session 2 you have considered the stages in the marketing planning process and how each of the elements of the process interlink to help retailers develop consisted marketing plans.

Session 3 focused on consumer behaviour and considered the marketing implications of the influences that affect how consumers behave.

In this study session, we have explored how branding is used in the retail industry and the concept of own-label brands. You were introduced to an academic literature review, which has distilled important works on retail branding.

In Block 4 you will study the supply chain, buying, and how goods get from the manufacturer to the shop floor.

References

Ackoff, R. I. (1987) 'Mission statements', *Planning Review*, vol. 15, no. 4, pp. 30–2.

Ailawadi, K. L and Keller, K. L. (2004) 'Understanding retail branding: conceptual insights and research priorities' *Journal of Retailing*, vol. 80, pp. 331–42.

Blackwell, R. D., Miniard P. W. and Engel J. F. (2005) *Consumer Behaviour*, Orlando, Dryden.

Bonoma (1985) *The Marketing Edge: Marketing Strategies Work*, New York, The Free Press.

Dennis, B., Neck, C. P. and Goldsby, M. (1997) 'Body Shop International: an exploration of corporate and social responsibility', *Management Decision*, vol. 36, no. 10, pp. 649–53.

Dunne, D. and Narasimhan, C. (1999) 'The new appeal of private labels', *Harvard Business Review*, vol. 77, no. 3, pp. 41–52.

Jennison, P. (1997) 'The new professionalism in retailing', *European Retail Digest*, vol. 14, (spring), pp. 11–13.

Jobber, D. (2010) *Principles and Practice of Marketing* (6th edn), London, McGraw-Hill.

Kassarjian, H. H. (1971) 'Personality and consumer behaviour economics: a review', *Journal of Marketing Research*, vol. 8, no. 4, pp. 409–18.

Maslow, A. H. (1954) *Motivation and Personality*, New York, Harper and Row, pp. 80–106.

McGoldrick, P. (2002) *Retail Marketing* (2nd edn), Maidenhead, McGraw-Hill Education.

Nielsen (2008) *Grocery Store Choice & Value for Money: A Global Nielsen Consumer Report* [online], http://no.nielsen.com/site/documents/Nielsen_StoreChoice_ValueReport_Dec07.pdf (Accessed 14 February 2011).

Piercy, N. (2008) *Market-led Change: Transforming the Process of Going to Market*, Oxford, Butterworth Heinemann.

Piercy N. and Alexander, N. (1988) 'The status quo of the marketing organisation in UK retailing: a neglected phenomenon', *Service Industries Journal*, vol. 8, no. 2, pp. 155–75.

Pilcher, J. (2008) *Consumer Targeting in Food and Drinks: Lifestyle Brands, Personalized Nutrition and Customized Flavors*, London, Business Insights.

Singh, S. (2008) 'Is India the gateway to global domination for Tesco?' *Marketing Week,* 21 August.

Taylor, D. (2007) 'Never mind the sizzle … where's the sausage?', *Market Leader*, (winter), pp. 2–6.

Varley, R. and Rafiq, M. (2004) *Principles of Retail Management,* Basingstoke, Palgrave Macmillan.

Ailawadi and Keller references

Given below is a list of the references used in the article by Ailawadi and Keller, K. L. 'Understanding retail branding: conceptual insights and research priorities' from the *Journal of Retailing* which is set out in its entirety in Session 4 of this book.

Aaker, 1991 David A. Aaker, *Managing brand equity*, Free Press, New York (1991).

Aaker, 1996 David A. Aaker, Measuring brand equity across products and markets, *California Management Review* 38 (1996) (Spring), pp. 102–120.

Aaker and Keller, 1990 David A. Aaker and Kevin Lane Keller, Consumer evaluations of brand extensions, *Journal of Marketing* 54 (1990) (1), pp. 27–41.

Achabal et al., 1982 Dale Achabal, W. L. Gorr and Vijay Mahajan, MULTILOC: A multiple store location decision model, *Journal of Retailing* 58 (1982) (Summer), pp. 5–25.

Ahluwalia and Gürhan-Canli, 2000 Rohini Ahluwalia and Zeynep Gürhan-Canli, The effects of extensions on the family brand name: An accessibility-diagnosticity perspective, *Journal of Consumer Research* 27 (2000) (December), pp. 371–381.

Ailawadi et al., 1995 Kusum L. Ailawadi, Norm Borin and Paul Farris, Market power and performance: A cross-industry analysis of manufacturers and retailers, *Journal of Retailing* 71 (1995) (3), pp. 211–248.

Ailawadi et al., 2001 Kusum L. Ailawadi, Karen Gedenk and Scott Neslin, Pursuing the value conscious consumer: Private labels versus national brand promotions, *Journal of Marketing* 65 (2001) (January) (1), pp. 71–89.

Ailawadi and Harlam, 2004 Kusum L. Ailawadi and Bari Harlam, An empirical analysis of the determinants of retail margins: The role of store brand share, *Journal of Marketing* 68 (2004) (1), pp. 147–166.

Ailawadi et al., 2003 Kusum L. Ailawadi, Donald Lehmann and Scott Neslin, Revenue premium as an outcome measure of brand equity, *Journal of Marketing* 67 (2003) (October) (4), pp. 1–17.

Alba et al., 1994 Joseph Alba, Susan Broniarczyk, Terence Shimp and Joel Urbany, The influence of prior beliefs, frequency cues, and magnitude cues on consumers' perceptions of comparative price data, *Journal of Consumer Research* 21 (1994), pp. 219–235.

Baker et al., 2002 Julie Baker, A. Parsuraman, Dhruv Grewal and Glenn B. Voss, The influence of multiple store environment cues on perceived merchandise value and patronage intentions, *Journal of Marketing* 66 (2002) (April), pp. 120–141.

Bell et al., 1998 David Bell, Teck-Hua Ho and Christopher Tang, Determining where to shop: Fixed and variable costs of shopping, *Journal of Marketing Research* 35 (1998) (August), pp. 352–369.

Bell and Lattin, 1998 David Bell and James M. Lattin, Shopping behavior and consumer response to retail price format: Why large basket shoppers prefer EDLP, *Marketing Science* 17 (1998) (1), pp. 66–88.

Bellizzi et al., 1983 Joseph Bellizzi, Ayn Crowley and Ronald Hasty, The effects of color in store design, *Journal of Retailing* 59 (1983) (Spring), pp. 21–45.

Boatwright and Nunes, 2001 Peter Boatwright and Joseph C. Nunes, Reducing assortment: An attribute-based approach, *Journal of Marketing* 65 (2001) (July), pp. 50–63.

Broniarczyk et al., 1998 Susan Broniarczyk, Wayne Hoyer and Leigh McAlister, Consumers' perceptions of the assortment offered in a grocery category: The impact of item reduction, *Journal of Marketing Research* 35 (1998) (May), pp. 166–176.

Brown, 1969 F.E. Brown, Price image versus price reality, *Journal of Marketing Research* 6 (1969) (May), pp. 185–191.

Bucklin and Lattin, 1992 Randolph Bucklin and James Lattin, A model of product category competition among grocery retailers, *Journal of Retailing* 68 (1992) (Fall), pp. 271–293.

Corstjens and Lal, 2000 Marcel Corstjens and Rajiv Lal, Building store loyalty through private labels, *Journal of Marketing Research* 37 (2000) (August), pp. 281–291.

Danneels, 2003 Erwin Danneels, Tight-loose coupling with customers: The enactment of customer orientation, *Strategic Management Journal* 24 (2003), pp. 559–576.

Dawar and Anderson, 1994 Niraj Dawar and Paul F. Anderson, The effects of order and direction on multiple brand extensions, *Journal of Business Research* 30 (1994), pp. 119–129.

Desai and Talukdar, 2003 Kalpesh Kaushik Desai and Debabrata Talukdar, Relationship between product groups' price perceptions, shopper's basket size, and grocery store's overall store price image, *Psychology and Marketing* 20 (2003) (10), pp. 903–933.

Dhar and Hoch, 1997 Sanjay K. Dhar and Stephen J. Hoch, Why store brand penetration varies by retailer, *Marketing Science* 16 (1997), pp. 208–227.

Dickson and Sawyer, 1990 Peter R. Dickson and Alan G. Sawyer, The price knowledge and search of supermarket shoppers, *Journal of Marketing* 54 (1990) (3), pp. 42–53.

Donthu and Rust, 1989 Naveen Donthu and Roland T. Rust, Estimating geographic customer densities using kernel density estimation, *Marketing Science* 8 (1989) (Spring), pp. 191–203.

Dreze et al., 1994 Xavier Dreze, Stephen J. Hoch and Mary E. Purk, Shelf management and space elasticity, *Journal of Retailing* 70 (1994) (4), pp. 301–326.

Dubin, 1998 Jeffrey A. Dubin, The demand for branded and unbranded products: An econometric method for valuing intangible assets, *Studies in consumer demand: Econometric methods applied to market data*, Kluwer Publishers, Norwell, MA (1998).

Dunne and Narasimhan, 1999 David Dunne and Chakravarthi Narasimhan, The new appeal of private labels, *Harvard Business Review* 77 (1999) (May/June) (3), pp. 41–48.

Eroglu and Machleit, 1990 Sevgin Eroglu and Karen Machleit, An empirical study of retail crowding: Antecedents and consequences, *Journal of Retailing* 62 (1990) (Winter), pp. 346–363.

Farquhar and Herr, 1993 Peter H. Farquhar and Paul M. Herr, The dual structure of brand associations. In: David A. Aaker and Alexander L. Biel, Editors, *Brand equity and advertising: Advertising's role in building strong brands*, Lawrence Erlbaum Associates, Inc., Hillsdale, NJ (1993), pp. 263–277.

Ghosh and Craig, 1983 A. Ghosh and C. Samuel Craig, Formulating retail location strategy in a changing environment, *Journal of Marketing* 47 (1983) (Summer), pp. 56–66.

Greenleaf and Lehmann, 1995 Eric Greenleaf and Donald Lehmann, Reasons for substantial delay in consumer decision making, *Journal of Consumer Research* 22 (1995), pp. 186–199.

Grewal et al., 2003 Dhruv Grewal, Julie Baker, Michael Levy and Glenn B. Voss, The effects of wait expectations and store atmosphere evaluations on patronage intentions in service-intensive retail stores, *Journal of Retailing* 79 (2003) (4), pp. 259–268.

Gürhan-Canli and Maheswaran, 1998 Zeynep Gürhan-Canli and D. Maheswaran, The effects of extensions on brand name dilution and enhancement, *Journal of Marketing Research* 35 (1998) (November), pp. 464–473.

Ho et al., 1998 Teck-Hua Ho, Christopher Tang and David Bell, Rational shopping behavior and the option value of variable pricing, *Management Science* 44 (1998) (12, Part 2 of 2), pp. S145–S160.

Hoch, 1996 Stephen J. Hoch, How should national brands think about private labels?, *Sloan Management Review* 37 (1996) (2), pp. 89–102.

Hoch and Banerji, 1993 Stephen J. Hoch and Shumeet Banerji, When do private labels succeed?, *Sloan Management Review* 34 (1993) (Summer), pp. 57–67.

Hoch et al., 1999 Stephen J. Hoch, Eric Bradlow and Brain Wansink, The variety of an assortment, *Marketing Science* 18 (1999), pp. 527–546.

Huff, 1966 David L. Huff, A programmed solution for approximating an optimum retail location, *Land Economics* 42 (1966) (9 August), pp. 293–303.

Inman et al., 2004 J. Jeffrey Inman, Venkatesh Shankar and Roselline Ferraro, The roles of channel-category associations and geodemographics in channel patronage, *Journal of Marketing* 68 (2004) (2), pp. 51–71.

Iyengar and Lepper, 2000 Sheena S. Iyengar and Mark R. Lepper, When choice is demotivating: Can one desire too much of a good thing?, *Journal of Personality and Social Psychology* 79 (2000) (December), pp. 995–1006.

Jacoby and Mazursky, 1984 Jacob Jacoby and David Mazursky, Linking brand and retailer images: Do the potential risks outweigh the potential benefits?, *Journal of Retailing* 60 (1984) (2), pp. 105–122.

Jap, 1993 Sandy D. Jap, An examination of the effects of multiple brand extensions on the brand concept. In: Leigh McAlister and Michael L. Rothschild, Editors, *Advances in consumer research*, vol. 20 (1993), pp. 607–611.

Kahn and Lehmann, 1991 Barbara E. Kahn and Donald R. Lehmann, Modeling choice among assortments, *Journal of Retailing* 67 (1991) (3), pp. 274–299.

Kahn and Wansink, 2004 Barbara E. Kahn and Brian Wansink, The influence of assortment structure on perceived variety and consumption quantities, *Journal of Consumer Research* 30 (2004) (March), pp. 519–533.

Keller, 1993 Kevin L. Keller, Conceptualizing, measuring, and managing customer-based brand equity, *Journal of Marketing* 57 (1993) (January) (1), pp. 1–22.

Keller, 2003 Kevin L. Keller, *Strategic brand management: Building, measuring, and managing brand equity* (second ed.), Prentice-Hall, Upper Saddle River, NJ (2003).

Keller and Aaker, 1992 Kevin L. Keller and David Aaker, The effects of sequential introduction of brand extensions, *Journal of Marketing Research* 29 (1992) (February), pp. 35–50.

Keller and Lehmann, 2002 Keller, Kevin L. and Lehmann, Donald R. (2002). *The brand value chain: Linking strategic and financial performance* (Tuck School Working Paper). Dartmouth College, NH: Hanover.

Kumar and Leone, 1988 V. Kumar and Robert P. Leone, Measuring the effect of retail store promotions on brand and store substitution, *Journal of Marketing Research* 25 (1988) (May) (2), pp. 178–185.

Laaksonen and Reynolds, 1994 H. Laaksonen and J. Reynolds, Own brands in food retailing across Europe, *Journal of Brand Management* 2 (1994) (1), pp. 37–46.

Lindquist, 1974 Jay D. Lindquist, Meaning of image, *Journal of Retailing* 50 (1974) (Winter), pp. 29–38.

Mazursky and Jacoby, 1986 David Mazursky and Jacob Jacoby, Exploring the development of store images, *Journal of Retailing* 62 (1986) (Summer) (2), pp. 145–165.

McAlister and Pessemier, 1982 Leigh McAlister and Edgar Pessemier, Variety seeking behavior: An interdisciplinary review, *Journal of Consumer Research* 9 (1982) (3), pp. 311–322.

Mehrabian and Russell, 1974 A. Mehrabian and James A. Russell, *An approach to environmental psychology*, MIT Press, Cambridge, MA (1974).

Messinger and Narasimhan, 1997 Paul R. Messinger and Chakravarthi Narasimhan, A model of retail formats based on consumers' economizing on shopping time, *Marketing Science* 16 (1997) (1), pp. 1–23.

Meyers-Levy, 1989 Joan Meyers-Levy, The influence of a brand name's association set size and word frequency on brand memory, *Journal of Consumer Research* 16 (1989) (September), pp. 197–207.

Meyvis and Janiszewski, 2004 Tom Meyvis and Janiszewski Chris, When are broader brands stronger brands? An accessibility perspective on the success of brand extensions, *Journal of Consumer Research* 31 (2004) (2, September), pp. 346–357.

Milliman, 1982 Ronald E. Milliman, Using background music to affect the behavior of supermarket shoppers, *Journal of Marketing* 46 (1982) (Summer), pp. 86–91.

Mills, 1995 David E. Mills, Why retailers sell private labels, *Journal of Economics and Management Strategy* 4 (1995) (Fall) (3), pp. 509–528.

Monroe and Lee, 1999 Kent Monroe and A. Y. Lee, Remembering versus knowing: Issues in buyers' processing of price information, *Journal of the Academy of Marketing Science* 27 (1999), pp. 207–225.

Narasimhan and Wilcox, 1998 Chakravarthi Narasimhan and Ronald Wilcox, Private labels and the channel relationship: A cross-category analysis, *Journal of Business* 71 (1998) (4), pp. 573–600.

Nowlis and Simonson, 1997 Stephen Nowlis and Itamar Simonson, Attribute-task compatibility as a determinant of consumer preference reversals, *Journal of Marketing Research* 34 (1997) (May), pp. 205–218.

Park and Srinivasan, 1994 Chan Su Park and V. Srinivasan, A survey-based method for measuring and understanding brand equity and its extendibility, *Journal of Marketing Research* 31 (1994) (May), pp. 271–288.

Rangaswamy et al., 1993 Arvind Rangaswamy, Raymond R. Burke and Terence A. Oliva, Brand equity and the extendibility of brand names, *International Journal of Research in Marketing* 10 (1993) (3), pp. 61–75.

Richardson et al., 1996 Paul Richardson, Arun K. Jain and Alan Dick, The influence of store aesthetics on evaluation of private label brands, *The Journal of Product and Brand Management* 5 (1996) (1), pp. 19–27.

Sayman et al., 2002 Serdar Sayman, Stephen Hoch and Jagmohan Raju, Positioning of store brands, *Marketing Science* 21 (2002) (4), pp. 129–141.

Schlosser, 1998 Ann E. Schlosser, Applying the functional theory of attitudes to understanding the influence of store atmosphere on store inferences, *Journal of Consumer Psychology* 7 (1998) (4), pp. 345–369.

Schmitt, 1999 Bernd H. Schmitt, *Experiential marketing: How to get customers to sense feel, think, act and relate to your company and brands*, Free Press (1999).

Schmitt, 2003 Bernd H. Schmitt, *Customer experience management: A revolutionary approach to connecting with your customers*, John Wiley & Sons (2003).

Sethuraman, 1992 Sethuraman, Raj. (1992). *Understanding cross-category differences in private label shares of grocery products* (Marketing Science Institute Working Paper, Report No. 92-128).

Sethuraman, 2000 Sethuraman, Raj. (2000). *What makes consumers pay more for national brands than for private labels: Image or quality?* (Marketing Science Institute Paper Series, Report No. 00-110).

Sethuraman, 2002 Sethuraman, Raj. (2002). *Positioning store brands against national brands: To get close or keep a distance* (Working Paper). Southern Methodist University.

Sethuraman and Cole, 1997 Sethuraman, Raj, & Cole Catherine. (1997). *Why do consumers pay more for national brands than for private labels?* (Working Paper, Report No. 97-126). Marketing Science Institute.

Simmons et al., 2000 Carolyn Simmons, Barara Bickart and Lauranne Buchanan, Leveraging equity across the brand portfolio, *Marketing Letters* 11 (2000) (3), pp. 210–220.

Simonson, 1999 Itamar Simonson, The effect of product assortment on buyer preferences, *Journal of Retailing* 75 (1999) (3), pp. 347–370.

Simonson and Tversky, 1992 Itamar Simonson and Amos Tversky, Choice in context: Tradeoff contrast and extremeness aversion, *Journal of Marketing Research* 29 (1992) (August), pp. 281–295.

Steenkamp and Dekimpe, 1997 Jan-Benedict Steenkamp and Marnik Dekimpe, The increasing power of private labels: Building loyalty and market share, *Long Range Planning* 30 (1997) (6), pp. 917–930.

Steiner, 1993 Robert L. Steiner, The inverse association between the margins of manufacturers and retailers, *Review of Industrial Organization* 8 (1993), pp. 717–740.

Tversky and Shafir, 1992 Amos Tversky and Eldar Shafir, Choice under conflict: The dynamics of deferred decision, *Psychological Science* 6 (1992) (November), pp. 358–361.

Walters, 1991 Rockney Walters, Assessing the impact of retail price promotions on product substitution, complementary purchase, and interstore sales displacement, *Journal of Marketing* 55 (1991, April) (2), pp. 17–28.

Acknowledgements

Text

Jobber, D. (2010) 'Other promotional mix methods', *Principles and Practice of Marketing*, sixth edition, 2010, McGraw-Hill Higher Education. Copyright © 2010 by McGraw-Hill Education (UK) Limited.

Jobber, D. (2010) 'Marketing in the modern organisation', *Principles and Practice of Marketing*, sixth edition, 2010, McGraw-Hill Higher Education. Copyright © 2010 by McGraw-Hill Education (UK) Limited.

Taylor, D. (2007) 'Never mind the sizzle… where's the sausage?', *Market Leader*. Copyright © 2007 Warc.

Varley, R. and Rafiq, M. (2003) 'Retail brands', *Principles of Retail Management*, published 2003, Palgrave MacMillan. Reproduced with permission of Palgrave MacMillan.

Ailawadi, K. L. and Keller, K. L. (2004) 'Understanding retail branding: conceptual insights and research priorities', *Journal of Retailing*, vol. 80, pp. 331–342. Copyright © 2004 New York University. Published by Elsevier.

Figures

Figure 2.1, 2.2, 2.3, 2.4, 2.5, 3.2a and 3.2b: Jobber, D. (2010) *Principles and Practice of Marketing*, sixth edition, 2010, McGraw-Hill Higher Education. Copyright © 2010 by McGraw-Hill Education (UK) Limited. Reproduced with the kind permission of The McGraw-Hill Companies. All rights reserved

Figure 3.2a and 3.2b: Jobber, D. (2010) *Principles and Practice of Marketing*, sixth edition, 2010, McGraw-Hill Higher Education. Copyright © 2010 by McGraw-Hill Education (UK) Limited. Reproduced with the kind permission of The McGraw-Hill Companies. All rights reserved.

Tables

Page 49: © Fiona Ellis-Chadwick.

Illustrations

Page 5 left: Nitro Media.

Page 5 right: Provided by Nitro Media.

Page 7: © Fiona Ellis-Chadwick.

Page 13: Taken from http://blog.thebodyshop.com.au. Used under the Creative Commons License Deed 2.5 http://creativecommons.org/licenses/by-nc-sa/2.5/au/.

Page 18: © Peter Arnold, Inc./Alamy.

Page 19: © Imagebroker/Alamy.

Page 19: © Blickwinkel/Alamy.

Page 20: Courtesy of Jarcje at en.wikipedia. Used under http://commons.wikimedia.org/wiki/GNU_Free_Documentation_License.

Page 21: © Fiona Ellis-Chadwick.

Page 23: © Fiona Ellis-Chadwick.

Page 26 Artist's Pallet: © Adam Gryko/www.iStockphoto.com.

Page 26 Flowers: © Shirley Ellis.

Page 32: © CartoonStock.

Page 33: © Mirrorpix.

Page 34 Soft Scoop ice cream: © Catherine Yeulet/iStockphoto.com.

Page 34 Strawberry ice cream: © D. Hurst/Alamy.

Page 35: © Studioshots/Alamy.

Page 42: © Motoring Picture Library/Alamy.

Page 47: Courtesy of intangible Business Limited.

Page 49 top: © Airwair International Limited.

Page 49 bottom: © Microsoft.

Page 50 © Fiona Ellis-Chadwick.

Pages 53 and 54: Courtesy of The Advertising Archives.

Page 55: © Maurice Savage/Alamy.

Page 60 GranArom coffee: © Fiona Ellis-Chadwick.

Page 60: Courtesy of Asda.

Every effort has been made to contact copyright holders. If any have been inadvertently overlooked the publishers will be pleased to make the necessary arrangements at the first opportunity.

Module team

The Module Team

Fiona Ellis-Chadwick (Module Team Chair and author)
Caroline Emberson *(Author)*
Roshan Boojihawon *(Author)*
Leslie Budd (Reader in Social Enterprise, OUBS)
Michael Phillips (Group Regional Manager, Undergraduate Programme)
Frances Myers (Regional Manager)
Erica Youngman (Programme Coordinator)
Colin Stanton (Curriculum Manager)
Iris Widdows (Curriculum Manager)
Pat McCarthy (Qualification Manager)
Val O'Connor (Module Team Assistant)
Sue Treacy (Module Team Assistant)

Other contributors

Diane Preston, Open University Business School
Mohammed Rafiq, Loughborough University Business School
Keith Pond, Loughborough University Business School
Christopher Moore, Caledonian Business School

Critical Readers

Haider Ali
Kristen Reid
Sue Hughes
Joan Hunt
Sally Booker
Rob Parker
Jerome Kiley
Noreen Siddiqui
Terry Robinson
John Pal
Paul Cowell

External Assessor

Professor Peter Jones, Department of Business, Education and Professional Studies, University of Gloucestershire

Production Team

Jodie Archbold (Picture Researcher and Rights Clearances Assistant)
Jill Alger *(Editor)*
Martin Brazier (*Graphic Designer*)
Johanna Breen (Editorial Media Developer)
Anne Brown (*Media Assistant*)

Angela Davies (*Media Assistant*)
Vicky Eves (*Graphic Artist*)
Chris French (Producer for Sound and Vision)
Sara Hack (*Graphic Artist*)
Lucy Hendy (*Media Assistant*)
Diane Hopwood (Picture Researcher and Rights Clearances Assistant)
Chris Hough (*Graphic Designer*)
Lee Johnson (Media Project Manager)
Edwina Jones (Editorial Media Developer)
Jane Roberts (Producer for Sound and Vision)
Kelvin Street (*Librarian*)
Keith Wakeman (Online Service Administrator)

Video assets

Nigel Douglas (Executive Creative Director)
Robin Tucker (Head of Production)

Consultants

James McGill (Figure descriptions)
Paul Meakin (Adviser on Law)